LANGUAGE AND LITERATURE : DIVERS INDIAN EXPERIENCES

QAISER ZOHA ALAM

ATLANTIC PUBLISHERS AND DISTRIBUTORS

Published by
ATLANTIC PUBLISHERS AND DISTRIBUTORS
B-2, Vishal Enclave, New Delhi-110 027
Phones 5413460, 5429987

Sales Office
4346/4C, Ansari Road, Darya Ganj,
New Delhi-110 002
Phones 3273880, 3285873
Fax 91-11-3285873

ISBN 81-7156-586-7

Typeset at
APD Computer Graphics, Delhi

Printed in India at
Mehra Offset Press, New Delhi-110 002

To

MY WIFE

PREFACE

For the present work I have made use of the material contributed by me in the form of articles to journals. The book contains studies which have already appeared in anthologies also. However, they have been revised before inclusion in this book. The book contains six articles on Indian English literature. Though there has been a spate of academic critical activity in this area these articles will be found interesting and helpful. As the book contains several articles on Urdu literature and studies where English and Urdu have been compared and contrasted the teachers and students of Urdu may also benefit from it. The book contains a chapter on the influence of English on Kurmali (a tribal language).

It is my hope that the present volume may help to promote further fruitful discussion on issues connected with India, Indian English literature, Indian languages and contrastive analysis.

I am deeply indebted to the writers whose writings have been of help to me. Needless to add, I am solely responsible for any errors and imperfections that still remain in the book.

QAISER ZOHA ALAM

CONTENTS

Chapter 1

KANTHAPURA'S STYLE : A POINT OF VIEW

Kanthapura, a social and political novel and Raja Rao's first full-length work of fiction, tells us of the impact of mystical Gandhism on an Indian village. It satisfies, to a considerable extent, the demand that a novel in English by an Indian author must be Indian peculiarly and essentially. To give it its due, the novel comes up to this assumption also in another and more acute way. The language of the novel reproduces the speech patterns of Indians using English and represents the way Indians talk and think. To be more precise, one gets a clear sense of South India in this novel. Indianisms abound in it and this is not unnatural either. As we know, even Rudyard Kipling had the habit of literally translating the speech of the Indian characters into English. It is not expecting too much then that the readers of Indian writings in English will accept this kind of language — an acquired one expressing a distinctive Indian sensibility. As Narasimhaiah has observed : 'Here is a distinctive Indian sensibility, a peasant sensibility, to be precise, and expressed in the English language. The words are English but the organisation is Indian.'

There is no denying the fact that *Kanthapura* has been written in competent English that illustrates the writer's command of the medium. Although Kantak is of the opinion that 'an unfriendly spirit hovers over all our efforts at creative writing in an alien tongue', it would be readily admitted that Raja Rao tried, not unsuccessfully, to give us the 'feel' of the life in South India through the medium of an alien language and the marks of laboured acquisition are, by and large, conspicuous by their absence.

While reading *Kanthapura* certain things strike as remarkable —. quite some of them stylistically. In this essay I propose to share some of them with my readers. It should be realized that my aims are humble and I should warn my readers not to look for anything of great depth here. In particular, I will talk about and illustrate the expressions of Indian flavour as used in this novel (in many cases, Kannada flavour, to be exact).

The novel is interspersed with the minor details of the description of nature. These and many other passages in the novel, in fact, suggest that many things here have 'close affinities with poetry'. A not-too-happy-a-scene has been described thus :

> The darkness grows thick as sugar in a cauldron, while the bamboo creak and sway and whine, and the crows begin to wheel round and flutter and everywhere dogs bark and calves moo, and then the wind comes so swift and dashing that it takes the autumn leaves with it, and they rise into the juggling air, while the trees bleat and blubber.

The passage fully conveys the sense — and, what is important, it is one sentence.

The writer has frequently changed the usual pattern and the order of words, and constructed his sentences in special fashions. He has introduced his village, Kanthapura — 'High on the Ghats is it, high up the steep mountains that face the cool Arabian seas, up the Malabar coast is it'. To be exact, inversion is one of the techniques he has used repeatedly — it is natural with him, he does not do it consciously. The repeated use of the technique underlines Raja Rao's mastery of his medium also. The novel is crowded with expressions like 'Defend one must against evil'. As it often happens in the novel, this sort of transliteration verbatim gives the sentences a look which is strange but is not objectionable. For instance, he has a habit of intercepting the regular flow of the sentences and pitchforking the proper names in the middle or at the end : 'She was a pious old woman, Narasamma, tall and thin', 'She has never failed us, I assure you, our Kenchamma', 'From that day on they never spoke to each other, Narasamma and Moorthy', 'He will bring us the Swaraj, the Mahatma', and 'He's gone, Potter Siddayya'. In their contexts these look natural and lifelike. Besides, the images used also lend a poetic beauty to the novel. (To cite one instance,... 'white flame rising silk-like in the sun'.)

Though they may sound wordy to some the expressions like the following look attractive and grip attention :

> 'they turn now to the left and now to the right'
>
> 'he has said this and that'
>
> 'the peasants went into the ripening fields and led water here and led water there'
>
> — 'this girl and that'

— 'by this paddy field and that, and they would lift this hand and show that way and lift that hand and show this way'

— 'and he was turning to this side and saying something, and turning to that side and saying something'

— 'you will say we have lost this, you will say we have lost that'.

It is true, however, that we will not like the repetition of this trick again and again. Talking of his method of narration, another remarkable feature one notices is the repeated use of the conjunction 'and' which appeals to the ear and interests the readers. Raja Rao seems a fluent talker.

'—Then the Police Inspector saunters up to the Skeffington gate and he opens it and one coolie and two coolies and three coolies come out.'

Interesting way of stressing the massing up of coolies :

— and with more beating and more beating we fall back one by one against the earth'

A pathetic description which reminds us of Macbeth's 'Tomorrow and tomorrow and tomorrow' :

— 'with one man and two men three men and four men around'

— 'there is such a confusion that men grip men and men crush men and men bite men and men tear men, and moans on moans rise and groans on groans die out while the ambulance men are still at work and men are bandaged, and shots after shots ring out and man after man falls like an empty sack'.

Undeniably, the confusion has been communicated.

As Brunton has said, his old woman narrator (a grandmother) is a clumsy expedient, compelling him to write for pages at a time in a rigid syntactic pattern of short, hurried clauses :

— '... and he says, 'we are against all tyrants', and she says, 'Why, then, come to our village, son, and free us from this childless monster', and Moorthy says, 'we shall see', and she says, 'We ask you to come', and Moorthy says, 'I shall write to the Congress and if they say "Yes", 'I shall come', and then old Lakshmanna, who is a very clever woman, she says, 'Let us garland you,' and Moorthy cries out 'No, no', but she says this and that, and garlands him and says, 'you are my Lord, and though I saw you like a rat on your mother's lap, I knew you'd do great deeds and bring a good name to the Himavathy'.

This is, in fact, a very important passage since one finds here many of the notable characteristic features of Raja Rao's style. For showing repetitions in him I cite some more instances.

— 'The following Tuesday was market-day in Kanthapura, and we had risen early and lit the kitchen fires early and had cooked the meals early and we had finisned our prayers early'.

— 'Then we ate and we slept, and we spake and we slept and when they said, "stay here, sisters", we said, "we'll stay, sisters", and we settled down in Kashipura'.

Maybe the illusion created is not of living speech but such passages are not devoid of artistic and poetic worth. Many repetitions here as elsewhere in the novel remind us of epic repetitions ('Old Lakshmanna who is a very clever woman' she says, and 'But then you know, the tiger, his words were law in our village' are comparable with Arnold's 'Sohrab alone, he slept not'). Though full of overdone, tortuous repetitions and 'ands' some of these passages are indeed very fine ones. Let me illustrate this following sentence (Mind it, it is one sentence, again) :

— 'There are cries and shrieks and moans and groans, and men fly to the left and to the right, and they howl and they yell and they fall and they rise, too, to fly, but the soldiers have seen us, and one of them rushes toward us, and we are felled and twisted, we are felled and we are kicked, we are felled and the bayonets waved over our faces — and a long time passes before we wake and we find Stamma fainted beside us, and Madamma and I, who were soaking in a ditch, crawl past her'.

To be fair to the writer it is really a very touching description of the police atrocities on the crowd of the followers of Gandhiji. About passage of this kind Narsimhaiah has observed : 'The massing of words corresponds to the massing of men in a crowd and the massing of upsurging emotions in response to police treatment'. There is an un-ending stream of men entering into and coming out of the temple :

— 'People came and people went, they banged the bell and touched the bull and took the flowers'.

It is these examples that bring back to mind the well-known statement made by Raja Rao about the Indian way of story telling in the foreword to *Kanthapura*. According to B. Rajan : 'Perhaps the repeated 'ands' convey the excited volubility with which the Indians are said to express themselves as they rush and tumble and run on'. Rajan has also stressed, interestingly, that Raja Rao avoids here not only 'ats' and 'ons', also 'ifs' and 'buts'. Believe me, the following is only a part of a sentence :

— 'What should we see by the temple corner but the slow-moving procession of coolies, — the blue, pot-bellied, half-naked coolies, tied hand to hand and arm to arm — boys, old men, fathers, brothers, bridegrooms, coolies of the Skeffington Coffee Estate who had come to live with us and work with us and to fight with us —'.

Of course, it makes an interesting reading and reminds us of certain passages in Browning's *The Pied Piper of Hamelin.*

Another special feature is the presence of sonorous parades of proper names and Brunton's charge is not without some ground that most of the village folk here are little more than names.

— 'as Moorthy is being dragged down the steps Rachna's wife and Madanna's wife and Sampanna's wife and Papanna and Sankamma and Veeramma come forward and cry out'.

— 'then are camps in Seethapur and camp in Subbapur, and camps, too, across the Mysore border in Shikaripur and Somapur and Puttapur'.

Also, names have become descriptive :

— 'There is Waterfall Venkamma and Temple Rangamma and Patwari Nanjundia and Schoolmaster Devarayya — and then, of course, there's Bhatta'.

— 'from that day on Nose-scratching Nanjamma, and Post-Office-House Satamma, and Gauramma and Vedamma and I, and even Ratna, began to feel stronger and stronger.

However, to tell you the truth (incidentally, 'to tell you the truth' is Raja Rao's pet expression here particularly in the early part), these things may contribute to the artistic realization of the writer's intention, but they also give an unreal air, one which makes for a rhetorical and wordy style.

Like other Indians writing in English, Raja Rao also interpolates Indian words in English sentences. A social realist that Raja Rao is, we come across in his *Kanthapura* the Indian words like Maharaja, Howdahs, Sahib, Khaki, Bazaar, Charkas, Prabhat-pheris, lathi, Cummerbund, Badmash, Bunds, and Swaraj and compounds like Sahib-looking and Champak-like.

That brings us to an important point — the expressions of Indian flavour and tempo in *Kanthapura*. Depiction of the social mechanism as available in the India of the time, specially South India, being his aim, such expressions naturally crowd the pages of the novel just like the novels of Mulk Raj Anand. It is remarkable, however, that these appear as integral parts of the novel and not just forced and brought in artificially. That is why his style bears a clear stamp of his own, a style which cannot be separated from a sensibility pre-eminently Indian. It is in this context that Narasimhaiah has mentioned the language of the dining hall : 'Take only this much milk, just this much' or 'Take it Bhattare, only one cup more, just one' and says that the English equivalents would have been 'annoying' and 'ineffective' since they (the Indians) need coaxing. Instead of saying 'nip it in the bud' Raja Rao has said 'crush it in the seed' ('aesthetically offensive imagery in the Indian context), and he takes resort to 'He is my wife's elder brother's wife's brother-in-law' and does not say 'cousin' (which, in fact, as Narasimhaiah has also remarked, does not convey the exact nature of our extended relationship).

Many of these expressions carry the names of animals and such other objects, particularly the cow, usually considered as the embodiment of all virtue. This is the old woman's description of village boy, Moorthy :

— 'He was not like Corner-House Moorthy, who had gone through life like a noble cow, quiet, generous, serene, deferent and brahminic, a very prince, I tell you'.

By the way, Nagarajan finds the comparison 'a defiant simile'. Here are some other expressions of this nature :

— 'helpless as a calf'

— 'Father naga'

— 'He wanted me to be his dog's tail'

— 'every squirrel has his day'

— 'before the cock has time to crow three times'

— 'my little mosquito goes to school and if he is worth the milk he has drunk, he will read it out to us'

— 'they were a set of buffaloes fit to be driven with kick and knout' (the Indians)

— 'She is as hale as a first-calved cow'

— 'we think of nothing but the blowpipe and the broomstick and the milking of the many cows'

— 'A cock does not make a morning'

— 'I saw you like a rat on your mother's lap'

— 'you cannot straighten a dog's tail'

— 'he drives away the flies from his pock-marked face'.

These expressions are really fascinating and in their situations look well-placed. The following are some more notable examples :

— 'why do you seek to make our stomachs burn' (while praying to Kenchamma)

— 'a crow and sparrow story'

— 'our granary is empty as a mourning house'

— 'I lick your feet'

— 'you are as a sister to me'

— 'in the dark half of the Sravan month'

— 'thin as a bamboo and shrivelled as a banana bark'

— 'we are the lickers of your feet'

— 'a thousand and eight Rama-Ramas'

— 'he, frightened, beat his cheeks and asked pardon of Sri Kenchamma'

— 'well-like silence'

— 'Free man you may be in your palace'

— 'you have the tongue to ask that too?'

— 'Oh, do not leave us to eat dust'

— 'our eternal dharma will be squashed like a louse in a child's hair'

— 'this Government wants to eat up the food of our ancestors'

— 'the sinner may go to the ocean but the water will only touch his knees'

— 'an ocean of tears'

— 'he closed his eyes for ever'

— 'yet not a hair of his head was seen'

— 'with his week's earning at his waist'

— 'their money tied to their waists'

— 'not a palm-width of space lay bare'

— 'but we have only a loin-cloth width of land'.

Needless to say, all these have sprung directly from the peculiar Indian experience and the then prevailing situation here : they convey an Indian essence and the writer is obviously trying all the time to give an idea of this situation, this experience, in a foreign language. This feeling becomes all the more intense when one finds the language of the novel, like the language in Anand's novels, is rich also in its 'repertoire of abuse' — abuse with Indian flavour. The word 'whore', for example, seems to be a favourite with the writer. Then abuses thrown by Venkamma are specially noteworthy. She says about her sister-in-law, Rangamma : 'If her parents are poor, let them set fire to their dhoti and sari and die. Oh, if only I could have had the courage to put lizard-poison into their food. Well that will come too', Bade Khan retorts when asked 'Who's there?' with 'Your wife's lover' and 'you son of my woman'. These almost literal translations of the speech lend naturalness and an effect of verisimilitude. Virago Venkamma sneers at Moorthy : 'Ah this cat has taken to asceticism — only to commit more sins'. Moorthy's mother speaks disparagingly of Mahatma Gandhi and remarks : 'Oh this Gandhi, would he were destroyed'. When the wind lets them down, they admonish it : 'Oh, you prostitute of a wind. She is showing her tricks again. Stop, you bitch'. Let me illustrate my point further by citing the following muster-roll of abuses used in the novel. To be true, many of them are simple admonitions :

— 'and it is not her father that built it (the house) ... and that shaven widow hadn't even the luck of having a bandicoot to call her own'.
— 'you had better go to the Big Field and see whether those sons of concubines are planting well'.
— "then there is such a battle of oaths — 'son of concubine' — 'son of a widow' — 'I'll sleep with your wife' — 'you donkey's husband'.
— 'you ass' — you pig' — 'you devil' — and such shower of spittle and shoes"
— 'Stop this concubine show'
— 'Ah I've seen your elders, you son of my concubine'
— 'Concubine Chinna still remains in Kanthapura to lift her leg to her new customers'.
— 'a traitor to your salt givers'
— 'the licker of your feet'
— 'I am no son of a prostitute'
— 'brahminism is as good as kitchen ashes'
— 'I am no butcher's son to hurt you'

— 'they had better eat mud and drown themselves in the river'

— 'And our community will not be corrupted by such dirt-gobbling curs'

— 'he will get a jolly fine marriage-welcome with my broom-stick'

— 'you think the cock only crows because of you'

— 'not till I've poured my shoe-water through his throat'

— 'Oh, you bearded monkey'

— 'Oh, you pariah-dog'

— 'He was not my uncle's son, was he?'

— 'We shall eat mud and nothing but mud'. 'Yes', says I, 'if every bloke eats mud, I, too, shall eat mud. The laws of God are not made one for Range Gowda and one for Putta Gowda. Mud shall I eat, if mud I should eat'.

— 'And I shall not close my eyes till that dog has eaten filth' (Range Gowda says about Bade Khan).

— (Range Gowda says) 'of course, of course. And this Range Gowda has a golden tongue and a leather tongue, and what is uttered by the golden tongue is golden and sure, and what is uttered by the leather one is for the thief and concubine'.

— 'If you are the sons of your fathers...'

— (Venkamma says to herself) 'you widows, you will not even lick the remnant leaves in the dust-bin you polluted widows'.

— (then comes the roar of Waterfall Venkamma) 'Ah, you will eat blood and mud I said, you widow'.

— (Venkamma to Pandit Venkateshia's daughter-in-law, Lakshmi, who takes her lantern and rushes to Venkamma saying 'And what is it Venkamma?) 'Oh, daughter of the mother-in-law, what is it but that this pariah-polluter has had royal visit?'

— (the regular cry of Rangamma's mother) 'Oh sinners, sinners, to have this in our old age'.

— 'If you are not silent, you will get a marriage greeting today'

— 'you sons of my woman'

— 'Give them a shoe-shower'

— 'they are not your uncle's grandsons'

— 'If this Government's people were really sons of their father ...'

— 'Oh, when you strike a cow you will fall into the hell of hells and suffer a million and eight tortures and be born an ass'.
— 'if this Government cannot tell the difference between a deer and a panther, well, it will fall into the mouth of the precipice'.
— 'May this Government be destroyed'
— 'Oh, Goddess, destroy this Government'
— 'You rat of a woman'
— 'you sons of my woman' (uttered in a harmless way here)
— 'Oh, you polluted ones'
— 'feast for a polluted pig'
— 'Oh, you dogs'
— (The warders cried) 'Ass, Pig, Badmash'
— 'Butchers, butchers, dung-eating curs'
— 'Ah, you've come, my bitch, and your husband is in prison'
— 'we have slept the sleep of asses'
— 'The policemen are not your uncle's sons'
— '(Timmi is crying out)' 'Oh, The Bell-field, May your house be destroyed'.
— 'may your wife die childless — I'll sleep with your mother' And the lamentations begin and lathis strike and the shriekings die down.
— 'we rushed to see who these bitches could be'
— (the soldiers say) 'I say the fields are bought, you pigs'.

Isn't it an imposing line-up of the strange transplantations of idioms? These abuses and invectives are, in fact, in wide currency in the different lauguages of India. The massing up of them in the novel may as well indicate the frequency with which we use them in real life.

Another distinguishing mark in this domain is large scale use of the word 'spitting' (To be exact, the word has been used about forty times in the novel). Indeed, the word has shaped into a kind of image to display one's hatred for something or to abuse the thing or to show the police atrocities then or an emphatic disapproval of something. At times the expression does not show much of abuse — 'Jayaramachar looks just as though he were going to spit out, and we never saw him again'. Sometimes the act of spitting is actually there as a curse or as a mark of anger, hatred or as a punishment. Waterfall Venkamma spat into the street while abusing Moorthy. She spat at the door of Moorthy's house and walked away. Standing on the village gate, Narsamma spat once towards the east and once towards the west, once towards the south and once towards the north, and then, spitting again thrice at the pariah huts, where the dogs began to raise a howl, she ran. The maistri howled and spat at Madanna's widow Sankamma. Siddayya curses the rain and draws away his hookah and spits the south-west way. When nobody turns towards Rachanna her reaction is: 'Thoo, Thoo, Thoo'. Venkamma meets Rangamma and looking away she spits behind her. Ramakrishnayya comes when policemen are there and spits across the courtyard. Waterfall Venkamma spits on the house and remarks: 'Oh, this widow has now begun to live openly with her men'. Vasudev says that in the estate Bade Khan spits and beats everyone and Rangamma imagines : 'Bade Khan after Bade Khans, short, bearded, lip-smacking, smoking, spitting, booted Bade Khan'. When the Mahatma takes a handful of salt and his followers break the law the police have been shown dragging them and spitting on them. The man on the top spits down on Moti Khan in the toddy grove. Venkamma called these people the toddy people and spat on them. When Ratna is given a kick in the back she cries out, 'Oh you dogs' and the Police Inspector spits in her face. The policemen beat Puttamma's father because he had spat on the false Patel. Incidentally, the policemen have been repeatedly shown kicking the freedom fighters and spitting on them and also into their mouths. When Rachanna's wife can bear the sight of the police atrocities no more she spits once, twice, thrice towards the Bebbur Mound, and once, twice, thrice at the village gate. In Maddur also 'the policemen rushed to smite these people and they spat and they kicked and they crushed and they banged'. Significantly, the novel closes with narrator praying to Kenchamma and Siva to protect them and then she spat three times to the west and three times to the south.

As we know, spitting in an irregular manner is a nasty habit with many of us and also 'spitting' is often used as a sign of anger, contempt, and hatred. Many a time even if it is not present physically it is there as a suggestion. *Kanthapura* is also not without such instances. Jayramachar's story mentions 'men who have come from across the seas and the oceans to trample on our wisdom and to spit on virtue itself'. Range Gowda shows absolute trust in Moorthy : 'Do what you like, learned master. You know things better than I do, and I know you are not a man to spit on our confidence in you'. Moorthy suggests to the villagers that if the Patel or policemen or agent should enter the house they should 'take the sanctum bell and ring, and we shall know they are there and we shall be there before you have swallowed your spittle thrice'. This 'spitting' has been made use of as an effective image several times in the novel. Through the bath-room comes Moorthy's soft tap-tap like a lizard spitting. When Bhatta's house is on fire 'the byre spits out jets and jets of stifled smoke that curls over the ripening fields' and when the Skeffington coolies shout 'Inquilab Zindabad' a volley spits into the air.

It is more than evident that the English in novel (as in many other novels written in English by Indian authors) is quite distinctive — has an original colour, a recognizable mode of style which well presents ways of thought and feeling. The importance of all this needs to be asserted bearing in mind the fact that this novel was written decades ago and is an early novel in English by an Indian. Obviously, then this has been a pace-setter, something followed by the later 'practitioners' as a pattern. The various expressions including the abuses lend the novel an extraordinary look. This English has its own vocabulary, its own idiom, its own morphology, and perhaps its own syntax also (many things have been derived from the vernacular). A native speaker of English will find the reading of the novel a bizarre experience linguistically though the use of 'Ah' and 'Oh' again and again will be to his taste. At the same time, occasionally Raja Rao has taken liberties — 'native' liberties, so to say, with the English language (*e.g.* 'says I'). Many things here will admittedly go over the native speaker's head, the 'operative sensibility' being essentially Indian and a flavour of Indian life, the Indianness, being transmitted. Kantak has gone to the extent of observing : 'The transformation of language takes place at a high artistic pressure ... The language has shaken off all traces of foreign acquisition and begun to assert its inalienable rights as an independent idiom' (By the way, Kantak has made this remark about Raja Rao's short story, *Javni,* but the statement is equally applicable to *Kanthapura).* However, a native speaker, known for his characteristic understatements, and 'excessive caution' will find the abuses which crowd the pages here a novel experience.

Undeniably, the appeal becomes compartively limited and local but even then it is a good sign in this age of internationalism that the Indo-Anglian writing is being taught at many foreign universities. If one's approach is sociological a novel like *Kanthapura* would provide sufficient food for thought since much is communicated about the contemporary society through the novel. Although writing in a foreign medium the writer succeeds in showing himself up as a 'witness in time', one who depicts the contemporary society. A reader is supposed to learn a great deal more about India culturally and linguistically from a novel like this than from a book of history. 'Raja Rao has written in English', S. Nagarajan said, 'which is not one of the fourteen languages of the Constitution, but his novels are Indian because he has progressively evolved for himself a definition of India which gives a certain unity of purpose to all his work'.

I would like to emphasise, once again, that since a very serious effort has been made to use the formal English syntax to depict 'the moods and tensions', which go with Indians it is really an interesting experiment with the English language. In fact, it is the language used in such novels as these that gives a special tinge to the dialect of English, many call Indian English. At least it imparts to the language a freshness and vividness which even during a hasty reading one cannot miss. Also, the self-consciousness of the attempt is largely absent. Generally speaking, it would not be too much to say that Raja Rao has given the English language an Indian domicile (Mrs. Mukherjee has used this term for Anand). That the English language communicates the peculiar Indian experience is proof of its 'plasticity and flexibility' as will be evident from the numerous instances cited in this essay. Though *Kanthapura* is an early novel written by an Indian about Indian life (in English), Raja Rao, who was a struggling young writer then, did not find the difficulties inherent in such a venture insuperable. In fact, the infusion of the resources of different languages as borne out amply by the illustrations given in the essay, is quite an achievement in the task of exploiting a variety of Indianisms in an artistic manner.

NOTES

1. All references to *Kanthapura* are based on Orient Paperback edition.
2. M.K. Naik, S.K. Desai, G.S. Amur (eds.), *Critical Essays on Indian Writing in English*, Dharwar, 1968.

Chapter 2

TRAIN TO PAKISTAN — A STUDY

It is half English, half
Indian, funny perhaps, but it is honest.
It is as human as I am human, don't
you see?

This remark of Kamala Das on her poetry in English applies with equal force to the Indian English fiction and, for our present purposes, to the writings of Khushwant Singh whose first novel, *Train to Pakistan* (1956) I propose to take up for a somewhat detailed study here. The point of departure for our discussion will be the language and particularly the expressions with Indian flavour one finds in this novel. The fact that the study of language in a novel has assumed great significance these days need hardly be repeated here. *Train to Pakistan* won the Grove Press Award. It is a short novel running into 158 pages. The techniques used by the writer are narrative, conversation, and description. As for narrative he has adopted an omniscient view, an all-knowing attitude. Raja Rao's narrative technique in *Kanthapura* is 'I' technique — a certain character narrates and thus makes comparatively a large scale use of the expressions of special flavour.

Khushwant Singh moves forward quickly into the conflict of the state of affairs he presents. To be very true, the early part of *Train to Pakistan* makes a silghtly dull reading. In fact, many things (for example, the cliches like 'when all was said and done ...') in the language of the novel keep us reminding that the novelist who is a leading journalist of the country has not been able to give us a visionary writing. It should be emphasized, however, that this is a novel of a realistic kind where we find 'documentary and descriptive realism'. A perusal of the novel gives an impression that Khushwant Singh is not very far from being a 'news-bearing' novelist who is indulging in a kind of 'reporting'. But, to quote Ezra Pound, 'literature is news that stays news'. There is no denying the fact, however, that the story of *Kanthapura* has been told, from a creative point of view, on a higher level than the story of the village Mano Majra. *Train to Pakistan* lacks a sustained flight of imagination ('the train, which embodies the motif of life, is a ... dual symbol. On the one hand it symbolizes life and action; it stands for death and disaster on the other' — Shahane). Incidentally, the first two paragraphs of this novel also form the starting point of Khushwant Singh's essay *Why Hindu and Muslim Speak Hate* (in *Khushwant Singh's India*). As the novel advances, however, we find a lot more of such Indianisms. The long passage describing the advent of the monsoon creates an atmosphere and expresses a kind of poetic feeling. It seems that the monsoon is a pet topic with Khushwant Singh. One is reminded of his long essay *The Monsoon – Bharat's Varsha* to be found in his *India Without Humbug*, which, however, contains a big extract from this passage in *Train to Pakistan* (but the borrowing has been acknowledged).

It may be reasonable to say that *Train to Pakistan* is a combination of various strains. Humour, violence, cruel events and torture lend it a tinge of the 'picaresque' where Jugga is the anti-hero, — he 'plays a dual role of the creator and the destroyer' (Shahane). Though the novel tries to recapture a certain period in history yet it does not really possess many features of a historical novel. Thrills, excitements and suspense give it an element of the novel of adventure and the depiction of horror involving innocent people an appearance of a novel of terror. Undeniably, parochialism is also predominant — the novelist has chosen a certain locale and the characters display qualities peculiar to that area. Apparently, the novel defies classification, yet, as has been hinted before, it is basically a realistic novel. Shahane notes that it alternates between the dramatic novel and the novel of character, between growth in space and movement in time and therefore, simultaneously develops both of these dimensions. Interestingly, he finds the novel 'prophetic because it is so innately realistic'. The novelist, as Anthony Burgess once said, "identifies himself with the men and women of ordinary homes, streets, pubs, schools, prisons, using all kinds of language, flinching at no situation". I think I shall not be off the mark if I make the same statement about Khushwant Singh as he is seen in *Train to Pakistan*.

A significant feature of Khushwant Singh's writing here is that on many occasions, perhaps when he realises that his allusions are not intelligible enough, he puts the sense within brackets. To cite a couple of examples : 'Jugga is budmash No. ten (from the number of the police register in which names of bad characters are listed), and 'They are a race of four-twenties (Section 420 of the Indian Penal Code defines the offence of cheating)'. In Anand's *Coolie*, when the English Inspector of Police said, eyeing Prabha suspiciously, 'looks a bad character', Ram Nath remarked, 'yes, a rogue of number ten'. Though very occasionally but we do find a kind of repetition which is comparable with 'epic repetition' (*e.g.* 'He had just one child, this girl Nooran'). One readily grants that Khushwant Singh has a keen eye and observes things minutely :

— He (Iqbal) had seen Meet Singh's thumb, with its black cresecent of thumb.

— Iqbal walked in the shade of the wall of the gurdwara. Children had relieved themselves all along it. Men had used it as a urinal. A mangy bitch lay on her side with a litter of eight skinny pups yapping and tugging at her sagging udders.

—The lane ended abruptly at the village pond — a small patch of muddy water full of buffaloes with their heads sticking out.

—The party reached Chundunuger afternoon. The tonga came to a halt outside the police station, which was a couple of furlongs distant from the town. The prisoners were escorted through an arched gateway which had *welcome* painted on it in large letters. They were first taken to the reporting room. Just above the table was an old frame picture of King George VI with a placard stating in Urdu, *bribery is a crime.* On another wall was pasted a coloured portrait of Gandhi torn from a calendar. Beneath it was a motto written in English, *honesty is the best policy.* Other portraits in the room were those of absconders, bad characters and missing persons.

—Almost overnight grass begins to grow and leafless trees turn green. Snakes, centipedes and scorpions are born out of nothing. The ground is strewn with earthworms, ladybirds and tiny frogs. At night, myriads of moths flutter around the lamps. They fall in everybody's food and water. Geckos dart about filling themselves with insects till they get heavy and fall off ceilings. Inside rooms the hum of mosquitoes is maddening. People spray clouds of insecticide, and the floor becomes a layer of wriggling bodies and wings. Next evening, there are many more fluttering around the lamp shades and burning themselves in the flames.

There is poetry in prose fiction, as Allen Tate put it, and wherever you have narrative, fiction is poetry. A novel has been said, in a sense, to be a poetry of life. Khushwant Singh also exhibits this poetic insight, even if sporadically, in this novel :

— Pampas — stalk chicks hung on the verandah had been folded into large swiss rolls and tied between the columns. The stark white of the verandah was mellowed in the soft amber of the setting sun. The sweeper's boy lay curled on the brick floor clutching the punkah rope in his hand. His father was sprinkling water all around the rest house. The damp smell of earth mixed with the sweet odour of jasmines came through the wire gauze door.

— Twilight gave way to the dark of a moonless night. In the swamps by the river, frogs croaked. Cicades chirped in the reeds. The bearer brought out a hissing paraffin lamp which cast a bright bluish light.

— The sun sank behind the bridge, lighting the white clouds which had appeared in the sky with hues of russet, copper and orange. Then shades of grey blended with the glow as evening gave way to twilight and twilight sank into darkness. The station became a black wall.

— The northern horizon, which had turned a bluish grey, showed orange again. The orange turned into copper and then into a luminous russet. Red tongues of flame leaped into the black sky. A soft breeze began to blow towards the village. It brought the smell of burning kerosene, then of wood. And then — a faint acrid smell of searing flesh.

— The fire cast a melancholy amber light on the khaki walls of the bungalow.

To Khushwant Singh, as is evident from the above illustrations, nature is the background against which man lives. Significantly, many of the above quoted passages deal with ugly scenes and undesirable things but, at the same time, are not without a beauty of their own. The images that the writer makes use of in the novel also impart a poetic touch to the prose and awaken the reader's sensibility.

— The place looked like the scar of a healed-up wound.

— The sky was a flat stretch of slate grey.

— People empty their rifle magazines into densely packed trains, motor convoys, column of marching refugees, as if they were squirting red water at the Holi festival.

— Hukum Chand's plan became crystal clear as a day after heavy rain.

The comrade, Iqbal, whose name causes a great deal of confusion in the novel, often lectures and philosophises. Long explanations of his views appear as a hindrance because the reader wants to get on with the story all the time. There is perhaps only one instance of interior monologue in the novel and that monologue is Iqbal's. The description is spread into several pages, towards the end. When the reader wants to know the end he is kept from it by this long probe into the country of Iqbal's mind. But then since this is the single instance of such a monologue the novel has a lot of clearness about it.

Khushwant Singh had a hearty laugh at the cost of these 'comrades'. That he does not go all the way with them is apparent from his essay on Krishna Menon. At the same time he does not make secret of his contempt for the abominable gap between the rich and the poor.

— Poor villagers take their thirsty cattle out to drink and are struck dead. The rich wear sunglasses and hide behind chicks of khus fibre on which their servants pour water.

Without passing any judgment he succeeds without doubt, in asserting where his sympathies lay. Although a novelist does not need to be a social reformer, in this novel the social and moral concern of the novelist cannot escape the reader's attention. The social content is prominent and, in fact, one can say that the novel is a study (in sociology) of an incredible period. In fact, as is common knowledge, the very medium of fiction is 'life'. Some of the descriptions in this novel can be profitably compared with those in the writings of Naipaul.

We learn from his essay *English Zindabad* Vs. *Angrezie Hatao* that Khushwant Singh calls English his mother tongue because as he asserts, he is more familiar with it than with any other language. But the English as he writes betrays the interference of his other languages with it, that there is a constant gravitational pull, particularly of his mother tongue, is obvious enough. In *Train to Pakistan* he has used about 40 Indian words and many of them several times. For instance, he has used Sahib, Sahibs and Memsahibs. But we also get Inspector Sahib, Superintendent Sahib, Magistate Sahib, Babu Sahib, Deputy Sahib, Head Constable Sahib, Sardar Sahib, Sentry Sahib, Captain Sahib, Station Master Sahib, Lambardar Sahib, and European Sahibs. Other Indian words that we find in this novel are khaki, topees, kismet, budmash, punkah, muezzin, salaam and also salaamed, pukka, wah wah, wah Guru, pardes, loot, *nar admi*, chacha, Kalyug, Iqbal, kos (two miles), Sat Sri Akal, mullah, bhai, barah (Indianised form of 'Bearer'), huzoor, harey Ram harey Ram, hijras (hermaphrodites), bania (grocer), toba toba, hai hai, tamasha, zulum, achha, and sabash. The use of all these words has undoubtely heightened the social effect. Frequently, the local accent brings about 'mutation' in the form of many of these Indian words. Budmasha, budmashi, lambardara, Daleep Singha and Juggut Singha are clear examples. Whereas Raja Rao's characters exclaim 'Ah and 'Oh' in *Kanthapura,* Khushwant Singh gives this a Punjabi shade and we find 'Hai', 'Oye' and 'Oi' in his novel though Mulk Raj Anand often uses 'Ohe', 'Han' and 'Hai'.

As for Indianisms the novel assumes significance since it has a fair sprinkling of them and some of them are remarkable and make the reader think. To be exact, Khushwant Singh's characters often speak in the language they do in real life — there are instances of word for word translation, and he has been able to modulate the speeches of the various characters taking into consideration the social position and the circumstances of life. There is an attempt to make a wholehearted and unflinching description of the atmosphere of the countryside of the Punjab. Consequently, therefore, the language undergoes rigours and changes — too obvious to be lost sight of. Let me illustrate :

— Jugga's mother says to him. "Go. Go-wherever you want to go. If you want to jump in a well, jump. If you want to hang like your father, go and hang. It is my lot to weep. My kismet", she added slapping her forehead, "it is all written there".

— The girl (weaver's daughter) says to Jugga, "You put your hands on the person of a strange woman. Have you not mother or sister in your home? Have you no shame? I will also tell the Inspector Sahib that you are a budmash."

— "What has happened?"

"Ask me what has not happened?"

— "But how long can a smoke keep straight? There is crime in his blood."

— "Our poor food..."

— "... people sing his praise in the four corners of the earth."

— "Certainly, Babu Sahib", he said meekly. "I am your servant as well as that of the police."

— "May Allah be merciful. We are living in bad times."

— "Yes, Chacha – this is kalyug, the dark age."

— "Sahib's bed has not been laid yet ... would Huzoor like to sleep on the verandah?"

— "As long as he is there no one can harm a single hair of my head."

— "Toba, toba. Kill my own village banian? Babuji, who kills a hen which lays eggs."

— "Who will give his daughter to a budmash?"

— "Sentry Sahib, Sentry Sahib, Sentry Sahib", repeated the head constable angrily, "You have been eating my ears with your Sentry Sahibs. What do you want?"

— "... it will be us first and our wives and children before a single hair of your heads is touched."

— "the Sikhs and Muslims will be drinking water out of the same pitcher."

— "It did seem unlikely that an educated man will risk his neck for any cause."

— "What has been happening? Ask me what has not been happening?"

An aspect of the Indian speech habit is that frequently a parallel is made with money. Also, there are numerical assertions, again and again.

— "I've told him a thousand times ..."

— "You have seen the world and read many books, but take it from me that a snake can cast its slough but not its poison. The saying is worth a hundred thousand rupees."

— "He is one of a hundred."

— "Babuji, we are being polite to you. We keep saying 'ji', 'ji' to you all the time, but you want to sit on our heads. We have told you a hundred times we are doing our duty."

— "You have said something worth a hundred thousand rupees."

Now and then it appears that Khushwant Singh has carried this business of finding verbal equivalents to an extreme, and, if I am allowed to say so, some of them seem ridiculous. As for example, putting 'Government' for 'Sirkar' is something funny. One wishes Khushwant Singh had retained 'Sirkar' instead, specially in the wake of the fact that he has consumed a high dose of Indian words in the novel. It is quaint that he has mentioned 'Sirkar' in the essay on Bihar famine readily whereas here he makes it a point to translate the word into 'Government'. In Anand's *Death of a*

Hero : 'I have never seen a Sarkar run like this and you know how the Angrezie Sarkar has ground us down and made life as cheap as dust'.

— The young girl salaamed, "As you order."

— "Go to the Government." — "Go, the Government sends for you."

— "The Government is talking to you. Why don't you answer him?" scolded the old woman. "Government, the young girl is very shy. She will learn," she explains.

— "Government, she knows nothing about drink. She is hardly sixteen and completely innocent. She has never been near a man before. I have reared her for your honour's pleasure."

— "I am a humble bhai of the gurdwara and he is an emperor (Hukum Chand, the Deputy Commissioner). He is the government and we are his subjects."

— Now the Government itself had called her beautiful and was interested in her family.

— "The police are the kings of the country."

— "What honourable noun does your honour bear?"

"My name's Iqbal."

"May your Iqbal (fame) ever increase."....

"Where does your wealth reside. Babu Sahib?"

"My poor home is in Jhelum district."

"They said she was the Big Lord's daughter."

— "Of course, Chacha, whatever you say is right to the sixteenth anna of the rupee."

(Interestingly, Manohar Malgonkar uses burra-laat for big lord).

— "It is absolutely sixteen annas' worth in the rupee". Every rupee is worth sixteen annas, thought Iqbal.

— "We are your slaves, Mr. Iqbal. You should command us and we will serve you."

— "Has your honour been out walking in the rain?"

— "You should use your tongue with some discrimination. Mr. Iqbal. I am not in your father's pay to have to put up with your 'bloodys."

— "Sat Sri Akal, Babuji" he said. "I am going to be the servant of your feet. I will learn something."

— Sleep would not come to Iqbal.

Yet another striking quality of the Indianisms in the novel is the 'sonorous singing of praise' — another thing directly borrowed from the Indian speech. Needless to add, these are employed to flatter the vanity of the people of some status or in some vantage position. In fact, this loud singing is carried out to obtain some monetary or other kind of benefit from the person praised.

— "May your fame and honour increase. May your pen write figures of thousands and hundreds of thousands."

— "Cherisher of the poor, What does your honour fancy?"

— "King of pearls."

— "May your Government go on for ever. May your pen inscribe figures of thousands — nay, hundreds of thousands."

— "Your honour must be right."

"My honour is right," said Hukum Chand triumphantly.

Khushwant Singh has translated almost verbatim some well-known songs from the vernacular and used them in the novel. They bring a local and realistic feeling. Indeed, his aim all the time is to reproduce the very atmosphere he has been trying to describe.

— In the breeze is flying

my veil of red muslin

Ho Sir, Ho Sir.

— Sunday after Sunday, O my Life.

It would be in the fitness of things to describe the novel as a whole as 'a courtroom for the indictment of social abuse'. The so-called uncouthness, aggressiveness and vigour of the Punjabi expression and accent have been brought out in the rough and harsh but down-to-earth speech of many of the characters here specially the uneducated and rustic. Raja Rao has also made his characters utter abuses time and again but the abuses in his *Kanthapura*, for instance, appear notable for their comparative mildness when they are juxtaposed with the vehement ones thrown by the people in this novel. Significantly, not many of them are innocuous admonitions : 'It was not possible to keep Indians off the subject of sex for long ... No people used incestuous abuse quite as casually as did the Indians. Terms like *sala,* wife's brother ("I would like to sleep with your sister") and *susra,* father-in-law ("I would like to sleep with your daughter") were as often terms of affection for one's friends and relatives as expressions of anger to insult one's enemies'.

— "Open, you son of fornication, or we will kill the lot of you."

— "What these bangles, Juggia. Wear these bangles and put henna on your palms."

— "May Allah's curse fall on you."

— "That incestuous lover of his sister."

— "I suppose this has been put here by your uncle."

— "What seducer of his mother can throw bangles at me? what ..."

— "The Guru's curse be upon you."

— "We will get the story out of this son of a bitch of yours in our own way. When he gets a few lashes on his buttocks, he will talk."

— "Ass."

— "You are an ass of some place."

— "And didn't you see how that pig's penis spoke to Chacha? One's self-respect is in one's own hands."

— Jugga shakes and smashes Malli's head against the bars. Each jerk is accompanied by abuse :

"This is to rape your mother. This your sister. This your daughter. This for your mother again. And this ... and this."

— "May your mother die ... you son of a pig ..."

— "As for the Babu, for all we care he can sleep with his mother. Our problem is : what are we to do with all these pigs we have with us? They have been eating our salt for generations and see what they have done. We have treated them like our own brothers. They have behaved like snakes."

— "We first, then you. If anyone raises his eyebrows at you we will rase his mother."

"Mother, sister and daughter", added the others.

— "Get out, you bitch."

— "The officer rebukes Meet Singh — "... one should just let other take one's goods and sleep with one's sisters. The only way people like you will understand anything is by being sent over to

Pakistan: have your sisters and mothers raped in front of you, have your clothes taken off, and be sent back with a kick and spit on your behinds."

— "Well, if the village is not dead, then it should be. It would be drowned in a palmful of water. It consists of eunuchs."

— "What sort of Sikhs are you?" asked the boy, glowering menacingly. He elaborated his question : "potent or impotent?"

— Jugga's temper shot up at once : "That penis of a pig who sleeps with his mother, if he puts his root in Mano Majra I will stick my bamboo pole up his behind."

— "If it had not been for your policemen in their uniforms, I would like to meet the father of a son who could dare to bat an eyelid before Juggut Singh."

The novel contains several passages of romantic interest and, in fact, Khushwant Singh freely depicts a number of episodes concerning sex and, also, many of the abuses have a direct connection with it. But, why find fault with Khushwant Singh for this for, as the French say, "without adultery there is no novel."

Though not as often as in Raja Rao's *Kanthapura*, Khushwant Singh has also used 'spitting' as an image giving expression to contempt and anger. It has been shown twice just casually. Doesn't this underline the writer's desire to describe minor details?

— The young girl spat out the betel saliva and cleared the throat with a series of deep chesty coughs that brought up phlegm.

— "Thanks very much," answered Iqbal through the tooth paste froth in his mouth. He spat it out.

But the following illustrations from the novel present 'spitting' as a symbol of hatred and disapproval.

— Jugga held up Malli's head with both his hands and spat in his face.

— "... have your clothes taken off, and be sent back with a kick and spit on your behinds."

— "If I do not spit in his bottom, my name is not Juggut Singh."

— "If I do not spit in Malli's mouth, my name is not Juggut Singh."

It is not altogether unwelcome that the act has not been repeated again and again in the novel.

A novel deficient in humour lacks readability. *Train to Pakistan* is not without humarous and witty remarks. Khushwant Singh has rather a lively sense of humour and is hardly ever cold and prosaic. In fact, humour is part of his genius though his humour is not always sunny and genial. Generally, his targets are the oddities and eccentricities of the situations he presents and the follies and imperfections of the characters he portrays. One finds it difficult to check one's laughter when one watches how railtied the life of the people of Mano Majra is : they think and act in terms of the timings of the few trains that pass through the railway station of Mano Majra. The passages in which Khushwant Singh has decried 'the comrades' are also not devoid of humour. I cite the following as illustrations of humour in the novel :

— Jugga's arrival (in the jail) was the subject of much hilarity. "Oye, you are back again. You think it is your father-in-law's house," shouted one of the constables from his barrack. "It is, seeing the number of policemen's daughters I have seduced", answered Juggat Singh at the top of his voice. He had forgotten the unpleasantness of the tonga.

— "Oye, Badmasha, you will not desist from your badmashi. Wait till the Inspector Sahib hears of what you said and he will put hot chillies up your bottom." "You cannot do that to your son-in-law."

— "In disgust, he (Iqbal) turned to the matrimonial ads. There was sometimes entertainment there. But the youth of the Punjab were as alike as the news. The qualities they required in the wife were identical. All wanted virgins. A few, more broad-minded than the rest, were willing to consider widows, but only if they had not been deflowered. All demanded women who were good at h.h.a., or household affairs. To the advanced and charitable, c. & d. (caste and dowry) were no bar. Not many asked for photographs of their prospective wives. Beauty, they recognised, was only skin-deep. Most wanted to "correspond with horoscopes". Astronomical harmony was the one guarantee of happiness.

The above excerpt, however, seems not very relevant and exposes Khushwant Singh to the charge that he has not accomplished selection and rejection of details in the novel cleverly.

— Describing the storm and the destructions caused by it : All this happens in a few seconds. Before you can say *Chakravarty raja gopalachari,* the gale is gone.

— "Yes, I am Muslim, what else would Haseena Begum be? A bearded Sikh?"

Indeed, Khushwant Singh has told the story with vigour, humour and pity and has been able to present the physical horror. It should be noted, however, that he tries to grip and convey the moral horror also. His mode is not symbolism in the ordinary meaning of the word though the way the novel ends is symbolic. His style wherein small paragraphs, short sentences and simple structures predominate, has elements of precision and lucidity and is not without a grace of its own. Generally, one does not find the overdone, tortuous repetitions, long and convoluted constructions and mannered 'ands' of Raja Rao's style. In fact, Khushwant Singh has a good command of the local colloquial language and mannerisms. He brings a special flavour, as A.N. Jeffares has remarked about these commonweath writers in English (Jeffares mentions Khushwant Singh also) and makes 'a distinctive contribution to our common heritage'. It is true, however, that he often writes stiffly and pompously (Khushwant Singh says elsewhere — 'I endeavour to turn out a polished sentence which is at once pregnant with meaning and pleasing to the ear).' Khushwant Singh's language has a flavour of 'extravagance and flamboyance'. C. Paul Verghese thinks that *Train to Pakistan* does 'not rise far above the standard of sensational journalism'. But we need not come down too heavily on him for this — for can't we say that he has helped to revolutionize journalism by moving it into the precincts of fiction : is the novel a model of 'New Journalism' (which joins reporting with the techniques of fiction)?

To conclude : 'It is half English, half Indian, funny perhaps, but it is honest.

All references to *Train to Pakistan* are based on Hind Pocket Book : 1971 edition.

Chapter 3

THE IMAGE IN INDIAN FICTION IN ENGLISH : A NOTE ON INDIANNESS

Interestingly, the essential flavour in many images used by the Indian fiction wirters in English is Indian. In fact, their inherent Indianness cannot escape one's attention. Talking metaphorically or obliquely by implication is generally natural with Indians. In everyday language they often use imagery as a means of expression, reinforcement, endorsement, illustration, evocation and also as objective correlative. Indeed, their minds have a remarkable ability to shift gears smoothly from 'the literal to the fanciful' with a view to enhancing the possibility of wider implications.

True, a fine image from nature has been rarely lost sight of. Nature has, in fact, been a great fascination for Indian writers. It has been so with Valmiki and Kalidasa also. They have used nature for decorative purposes but over and over again it serves a function in the context as well. Many of these images appeal to the ear and many to the eye. Needless to add, quite a few of them are country pictures. The rivers have been again and again used as 'symbolic agents that purify the impurities of people who bathe in them, or even visit them' (Singh : 1977 : 199). For example, the Ganga in Raja Rao's and Sarayu in Narayan's fictional writings. The river Ganga is, in fact, a powerful cultural symbol. Narasimhaiah (1972) notes that such is the intimacy between man and nature that they even admonish the wind or the rain (in whom they have put their faith for their very existence) when it lets them down : "The prostitute of a wind, she is showing her tricks again" (*Kanthapura*, Raja Rao). Raja Rao's images come directly from the peculiar Indian experience and convey an Indian essence. Instead of saying, 'nip it in the bud', Raja Rao has said, in an Indian way, 'crush in the seed'. Raja Rao's *Kanthapura* is perhaps a miniature India – what swept over Kanthapura is actually what swept over

India as a whole during those years. ''Kanthapura is a symbol of India, past, present and future'' (Williams : 1976 : 49). We are reminded here of Bharathi Sarabhai's play in English entitled *The Well of the People*. The play presents the story of an old woman, a symbol of the misery and unhappiness of India. She saves a little money to go to the Kumbha Mela, but is unable to do so and spends her money in digging a well for the use of villagers. The old woman is, in fact, India.

Often when these writers want to compare and thereby create an image relevant to the scene described, they prefer doing so with the help of animal, bird or insect imagery. In particular, this kind of imagery has been often used as abuses and admonitions. Such dehumanizing metaphors which ascribe animal or inanimate properties to a human being, frequently have a ring of contempt (Leech : 1969 : 158). 'As if you were cattle/animal/beast' is an oft-repeated Indianism. 'I want you all to think independently, of your accord, and not allow yourselves to be led by the nose as if you were cattle' *(The Guide*, Narayan). When Raja Rao says 'like a noble cow', 'as a first-calved cow' and 'helpless as a calf', he is actually using variants of typical Indianisms. Many of these cow and buffalo images are, undoubtedly, Indianisms. 'They were a set of buffaloes' in Raja Rao's *Kanthapura*, is a plain Indianism. 'The Indian people' is the tenor of the metaphor and 'a set of buffaloes' its vehicle. We understand the metaphor as 'the ignorant Indian people are like a set of buffaloes'. As for the cat, the following one is almost a transliteration of a famous Indian saying — 'ah, this cat has taken to asceticism' (*Kanthapura*, Raja Rao). The Indian colloquial conversation is often replete with references to snakes, serpents and scorpions and the like. A good number of these images are auditory or acoustic — the sound under discussion is described as resembling the sound of the movement of the snake etc. These writers mostly use 'fish' in the sense it is colloquially used in many Indian languages : 'and you go like a fish hooked on a string, in spite of yourself' is a suggestive fish image in Joshi's *The Strange Case of Billy Biswas*. Many of Arun Joshi's images spring directly from Indian usage. Aftab Rai introduces Som to Gargi (in *The Last Labyrinth*) as a businessman whose 'touch could turn mud into gold'.

Generally, these writers tend to describe eyes the way they have traditionally been in Indian literatures. This from Joshi's *The Foreigner* appears a little stale as it is characteristically repeatedly used in India — 'large eyes were like a lake after a rain'. The fruit imagery comes handy when these writers think of female breasts. When Sonny's father, in Anita Desai's *Voices in the City*, mentions Jahanara's hair 'that came down the backs of her knees', he presents the sight, as is usually done in India, as 'that cloud of black hair swaying about the body'.

It seems that extreme hatred, helplessness, utter darkness, emptiness, silence and the situations of the like nature remind these writers of mourning, funeral, sympathy and such other things. Raja Rao mentions empty granary and is reminded of a mourning house; he mentions naked trees and thinks of widows before their husbands' pyre'. Narayan says in *The Financial Expert,* 'Why do you shout so much as if a great calamity had befallen the house'. 'Corpse', 'carcass', 'cremation' and 'dust' etc. are other pictures of this nature. Indeed, these writers have been often able to communicate the sadness and melancholy of the situation with the help of these images. Sometimes the images in these writings spring from religion-religious details or the things associated with religion act as vehicle or as tenor in some of these images. The mother in Desai's *Voices* is identified with Kali though not very convincingly and many say that she is really the goddess and the demon in one.

Spitting is habitually used in India to give expression to anger and also as a physiological and behavioural reaction accompanying it. It is often used in these writings and shapes into a kind of image to emphasize one's hatred for something or to abuse or ridicule the thing or to show atrocities or disapproval of something. In Joshi's *The Foreigner,* 'I was born an Indian and had been spat upon; had I been a European, I would have done the spitting'. In *Kanthapura* alone, the word 'spitting' has been used about 40 times. Spitting is often present as a suggestion, too. In *Kanthapura*, Range Gowda shows absolute trust in Moorthy, 'I know you are not a man to spit on our confidence in you'.

'Well' has been another recurrent image. Jagan, in Narayan's *The Vendor of Sweets,* talks about the people around him, 'people's notions were fixed, stupid fellows! Frogs in the well'. Many of the images, picturesque and detailed, emerge from the typical love and reverence for valuable metals, stones, glasses, ornaments and jewellery etc. Water often reminds Mulk Raj Anand of silver *e.g.*, 'the silver line of the Beas' and 'the silver line of a long water course' in his *Coolie.* Whereas Bhattacharya talks of 'each grain a grain of gold' in his *So Many Hungers*! Raja Rao wants the rice to be as fine as filigree in *Kanthapura.* Ahmed Ali remarks in *Ocean of Night,* 'Nawab looked as if he had won the pearls of the seven seas'. Ali's images, at least in his *Ocean of Night,* often appear literal translations from his mother tongue *i.e.* Urdu. In keeping with the prevailing atmosphere in the novel, Ahmed Ali uses images from classical music – 'thumri' and 'bhairon' etc. This picture of the fickleness of fortune has been perhaps borrowed straight from vernacular — 'how fickle is fortune, more than a woman's heart'. Talking of fortune again, Ali says, 'Fortune is fickle like the moon which lasts but only four days'. In the same novel, we have, 'Desire was restless like a moth around the flame' which, once again, is almost a literal translation of a well-known Urdu expression *i.e.* 'Shama' and 'Parwana'. Later, Ali talks of the 'feeling of the moth for the flame'.

Certain verbs as used by these writers have been transliterated from Indian language. It is interesting to note that such examples particularly abound in Anand and Khushwant Singh, both of whom speak Punjabi as the first language — 'you have been eating my ears' (*Train to Pakistan*, Khushwant Singh), 'you don't eat my head' and 'I will take you to eat a little fresh air' (*Coolie*, Anand). Anand's crude Indianisms often convey the essence better *e.g.*, 'I hear that the girl has rolled many papads' and 'you have cut my nose bitch' (*Old Woman and the Cow*) are interesting pictures and typical of Anand. According to Verma (1978, 1980), many expressions of this nature are not deviations but 'arbitrary creations' — "One might go to the extent of saying that in some cases they are bad translations ... they have been created in the process of finding translation equivalents of concepts and ideas deeply rooted in Indian culture, faiths and beliefs, of what the characters might have said in their mother tongues". Significantly, Verma (1980) is of the view that "their (the creative writers) creations are motivated by their desire to make English an effective tool of Indian culture". He feels that every creative writer has a right to explore the sociolinguistic resources of the language (s) he uses. Anand's statement is interesting (1969) : "I generally translate or interpret my feelings or thoughts from Punjabi or Hindustani into the English language, thus translating the metaphor and imagery of my mother tongue into what is called Indo-Anglo-Indian writing, but what I prefer to call 'pigeon Indian' (not Pidgin-Indian)".

An aspect of the Indian speech habit is that frequently a metaphoric parallel is made with money. Also, often there are numerical assertions ('lexical' or 'conversational' hyperbole). When used in these writings, they give them a more intimate local colour. The expressions of this nature are often resorted to in India particularly for emphasis. Khushwant Singh and Bhabani Bhattacharya have a special interest in such expressions — 'I've told him a thousand times', 'you have said something worth a hundred thousand thousand rupees' (*Train to Pakistan*, Khushwant Singh): 'you could do a hundred other things' ("Steel Hawk", Bhattacharya); 'You've got a hundred and one problems with your new whisky'

(*Storm in Chandigarh*, Nayantara Sahgal) and Gandhi 'will die a thousand deaths' (*A Bend in the Ganges,* Manohar Malgonkar). Many of the abuses and admonitions emerge from the characteristic Indian (or even regional) day-to-day conversations. For example, 'eater of your masters' (*Coolie*, Anand), 'lover of thy own sister' (*Ocean of Night*, Ahmed Ali), 'Ohe this Gandhi, would he were destroyed' (*Kanthapura*, Raja Rao), 'ohe, come on pubic hair' and 'son of a black Shaitan' (*A Bend in the Ganges*, Malgonkar) etc.

Social imperatives and traditions give rise to phrases, sayings and proverbs. Many of them have been unconsciously based on some kind of metaphorical use. Such idioms have also been called crystallised metaphors. To cite a few examples :

- you haven't the strength to kill an ant and will fight an elephant (*Ocean of Night*, Ahmed Ali).
- Toba, toba, kill my own village banian, Babuji, who kills a hen which lays eggs (*Train to Pakistan*, Khushwant Singh).
- He who has the big stick will have the buffalo (*Death of a Hero*, Anand).
- he was as yet essentially an ineffectual 'pawn on the chessboard of destiny' (*Coolie,* Anand).
- Bathe your feet while the Ganges still flows (*A Bend in the Ganges*, Malgonkar).
- Who gave the beak to the bird will also provide it with food (*A Bend in the Ganges*, Malgonkar).

Sheila said at one place in Anand's *Coolie*, 'Hot tea cools your heart in the heat of summer' — almost a literal translation of an aphorism very popular in India. The same can be said about this from the same novel — 'you have hardly a place to rest your head on for the night and you build castles in the air like Sheikh Chilli'.

Some of the images that we find in the Indian fiction in English apparently look stock, trite and commonplace uses, often indiscriminately used in our country and have hardened into cliches. Both Raja Rao and Narayan, for example, have used the expression that somebody 'is as a sister to me'. We have in Bhattacharya's *So Many Hungers*!, 'a golden lotus wasting in mud and filth', in Malgonkar's *A Bend in the Ganges,* 'The touch of the hand was like a flame', 'her fingers were like ice' and 'money was spent like water' and in Anand's *Coolie*, 'Why do you hide yourself like women'. As is often done in India, faces have been compared with flowers over and over again. These writers hold the lotus in high reverence. Aunt Alamelu in Markandaya's *Two Virgins* has been shown sitting 'cross-legged on the mat with her feet on her thighs, in the lotus position'. Sitting in the cross-legged position reminds them of lotus. The Yogi in the temple, in Anand's *Coolie*, had assumed the sacred posture of the lotus seat with legs crossed and hands resting like newly opened flowers. The fly has often been shown as a mark of ill-omen *e.g.*, in Anand, Joshi and Bhattacharya. Dropping of leaf or fruit easily or with a little shaking is another recurrent use.

Many similes and metaphors that these writers use appear attractive and evocative mainly because they have been transliterated into English from some Indian language. Some of these though not very fresh and original help the writers present the scene a little more realistically. Exaggeration is a quality shared by many of these writers and let it be noted here that exaggeration as a trait is common to many Indians. To my mind, what is most notable about their imagery is the inherent Indianness.

SELECT REFERENCES

Anand, Mulk Raj. 1969. A Plea for English for Higher Education. In : *Language and Society in India.* Transactions of Indian Institute of Advanced Study, Simla, Vol. 8.

Leech, G.N. 1969. *A Linguistic Guide to English Poetry*, Longmans.

Metaphor Research Newsletter, Adelphi, Vol. 1, No. 4, Vol. 2, No. 2, Vol. 3, No. 1, Vol. 3, No. 2.

Mohan, Ramesh (Edit.) 1978. *Indian Writing in English.* Orient Longman.

Narasimhaiah, C.D. 1977. *Moving Frontiers of English Studies in India*, New Delhi : S. Chand.

Singh, R.S. 1977. *Indian Novel in English.* New Delhi : Arnold Heinemann.

Verghese, C. Paul. 1971. *Problems of the Indian Creative Writers in English.* Bombay : Somaiya Publications.

Verma, S.K. 1978. Syntactic Irregularities in Indian English. In : *Indian Writing in English,* Ed. Ramesh Mohan. Orient Longman.

—, 1980. Swadeshi English : Form and Function. Indian Linguistics, Vol. 41, No. 2.

Williams, H.M. 1976. *Indo-Anglian Literature 1800-1970 — A Survey*, Madras : Orient Longman.

Chapter 4

THE IMAGE IN ARUN JOSHI'S FICTION

Arun Joshi has repeatedly taken resort to imagery in his fiction and says many things metaphorically. Some of his images spring directly from Indian usage and some from the contemporary life. It is easily noticeable, however, that he often draws his images from the darker sides of life. Joshi's first novel, *The Foreigner*, is drenched in imagery though the same cannot be said about his other novels. In *The Foreigner* , Joshi is preoccupied with 'different facets of the theme of alienation'. Sindi, for example, is a foreigner wherever he goes. Joshi's heroes — Sindi, Billy, Ratan and Som — are all 'outsiders' after a fashion, making desperate attempts to silence the insidious bug within and reach a rapport with the World (Iyengar, 1985, 748). *The Strange Case Of Billy Biswas* is a novel with myths and folklores with Billy as 'the archetypal hero, as a sort of mangod, an avatara to the tribals'. In *The Apprentice*, Joshi's 'vision of life, his compassion and sensibility are manifested in the archetypal patterns of conflict between good and evil'.

Arun Joshi's *The Strange Case* and *The Last Labyrinth* are not as rich in imagery as *The Foreigner*. 'Krishna', however, is an authentic symbol in *The Last Labyrinth* where the 'labyrinth' symbolism is spread out thick all over (Iyengar, 1985, 748). Many pictures in *The Strange Case* appear rather commonplace and some are more or less cliches. The following excerpt, however, is of interest :

— What was Bilasia? What is the playful effervescence of a mountain stream? What is sunlight frittering through a glade? What is the thunder of a volcano or the hardness of granite? What is the vengeance of a cobra whose mate has been killed?

Joshi's images are often integral parts of the context — in *The Apprentice* intricately interwoven in the fabric :

— For the Brigadier, as he remarked after joining the army, the world was a beautiful whore — to be assaulted and taken. To me, alas, it appeared as a bundle of mirrors, tempting and somehow held together, but on the brink always of falling apart, Or, like a boat managed by incompetent hands, a boat that could any moment overturn and drown its riders.

The musical images in *The Last Labyrinth* clearly show a tinge of originality : 'I had learnt another thing, one among the several cadenzas, simple and complex, with which I conducted my orchestras of discontent' and 'Why should she appear mysterious unless, possibly, there was a mystery within me that, in her proximity, got somehow stirred as one tuning fork might stir another'.

'Out of the blue', 'all said and done' and 'easier said than done', jargons usually associated with journalism, are often found in *The Apprentice* and *The Last Labyrinth*. It may be mentioned here, however, that even Maugham has made one of his characters say in his novel *Cakes and Ale*, 'When all's said and done, that's the only thing that counts'. Khushwant Singh has used this expression in *Train to Pakistan* and Mulk Raj Anand in *Two Leaves and a Bud*. In a journalistic vein, Joshi talks of the 'administrative fabric' in *The Strange Case*. 'Worse than (or less than) a beggar's shoe' is Joshi's image to express utter uselessness. The state of Ratan Rathore's father on the day he was killed and the procession that he led that day had been referred back time and again in *The Apprentice*. Also, it has been compared with the events happening presently in the life of Ratan, the protagonist. 'Filth' and 'bourgeois filth' have been used a number of times as images :

— How eager to tuck away the filth that is inside them

— Let me not fill your young ears with filth

Joshi has used figurative language also to give expression to political issues : 'Through the five-yearly farce of the ballot box' (*The Apprentice*). He talks of money figuratively : 'If I had everything and no money I would be little better than a beggar's shoe' — this is the approach of many in the present age and particularly of the new rich. Interestingly enough, in *The Last Labyrinth,* Som remarks, 'money was dirt, a whore'.

'Roaring' is an expression frequently used by Joshi (*e.g.*, 'the roar of her engine died' — *The Foreigner*). 'Roaring has been, in fact, a pet expression with many Indian writers in English. The figurative sense is related to the literal sense as they are related in certain ways. Like many of these writers, once again, Joshi, too, has used 'journey' as a metaphor.

One cannot miss the sharp and biting sarcasm in this statement : ''We did not learn to rub our father's gray head in dirt' (''Gherao''). ''When Mr. Khemka's industry is ruined, Sindi decides to leave for Bombay. On the departing morning the first monsoon shower comes. The shower is a fertility symbol, signalling the stirring of life in Sindi also'' (Prasad, 1985, p. 42).

Joshi treats nature as a dictionary from which he often borrows his images. Flowers and heavenly bodies particularly interest him :

— I stuck to vague generalities about Babu, giving her in driblets what she wanted in torrent (*The Foreigner*).

— uncovered sewers that roared after the day's rain like miniature rivers (*The Foreigner*).

— the moon-washed garden (*The Last Labyrinth*).

— It is an odd thing, playful and melancholy by turns, like the wind in a *saal* forest on a quiet afternoon (*The Strange Case*).

— my thoughts were still full of America which had forever slipped through my fingers like so much sand (*The Strange Case*).

— My chance of receiving help seemed to be trickling away like so much sand (*The Apprentice*).

'Like so much sand', it may be noted here in passing, has been an iterative image throughout the range of Indian fiction in English.

— the sea surf breaks on the island day and night forming a shimmering girdle of foam like the girdle of the moon (*The Strange Case*).

— If life's meaning lies not in the glossy surfaces of our pretensions but in those dark mossy labyrinths of the soul that languish forever, hidden from the dazzling light of the sun ... I know of no other man who so desperately pursued the tenuous thread of existence to its bitter end (*The Strange Case*).

— They blazed through the liquour-stimulated sensibilities, like little meteors through the astral night (*The Strange Case*).

— that summer stands out in my memory as one of my life's happiest periods, rather like a basket of flowers in a vegetable market (*The Strange Case*).

— One's youth when life is beguiling enough to present only its rosy face (*The Strange Case*).

Youth, as we know, has been often likened to a rose.

— it (moon) seemed to hang like an enormous flower in the inky space (*The Strange Case*).

— it had ... the clear stamp of a sorrow that seemed as out of place in a person like Billy as clouds on a spring afternoon (*The Strange Case*).

— the Billy Biswas I had known was finished, snuffed out like a candle left in the rain (*The Strange Case*).

— the gossip in the Delhi society was nothing short of a deluge, moreover, that continued to swamp us for many years to come (*The Strange Case*).

— the pious voices ... fell about me like waves of a benevolent sea (*The Strange Case*).

— Its (the moon's) light was everywhere, drenching the tree tops, softening the stone, bathing the bush with mystery (*The Strange Case*).

— He is like rains on parched lands (*The Strange Case*).

— You are not navigating by the stars (*The Strange Case*).

— The countryside exploded into a riot of colour (*The Strange Case*).

— a mountain crow black as midnight (*The Strange Case*).

'Time' has been used here for comparison. In *The Last Labyrinth,* Joshi talks of 'the blackness of my nights'. Incidentally, Ahmed Ali has described 'night' as 'this great negress' in his *Ocean of Night.*

— It is a confrontation whose outcome is as certain as the end of a solitary boat's beating against a maelstorm (*Ocean of Night*).

— There, look at those houses, cliffs in the night (*The Apprentice*).

Joshi finds "cliff-like houses" in Benaras (as described in *The Last Labyrinth)* :

— Some survive through defiance, others through ability. Some others through obedience, by becoming servants to the powers of the world. They are like those heavenly bodies that in themselves are nothing but reflect only the superior and more powerful lights (*The Last Labyrinth*).

— It (the vision of light) is there, like dirt caught in a storm (*The Last Labyrinth*).

— And enveloping all this, a fog beyond the fog (*The Last Labyrinth*).

— The confusion reduced me to the status of those leaves of autumn that are blown here and there, at the mercy of the wind (*The Last Labyrinth*).

— What significance was there in steering a boat that had as destination or watering a tree that would never bear fruit (*The Last Labyrinth*).

— I poured out words like rain (*The Last Labyrinth*).

— Beneath the placid waters of society floated the rest of the great mass which unknown men enacted day after day and got away with (*The Lasy Labyrinth*).

— The sun was already without mercy (''Gherao'')

an obvious instance of pathetic fallacy. The following is a good horticultural image : 'Boons are not given everyday, as though they were guavas' (*The Strange Case*).

As for animal imagery, sometimes Joshi does not mention any particular animal and instead uses 'animal' or 'cattle' as a concept or idea for the purpose of comparison : 'In her house she was like a pet animal which went about where it willed, confident of not being noticed' (*The Foreigner*) and 'When I see these young faces led like cattle'\ (*The Apprentice*). He mentions 'bull' in particular : 'Like a contracted bull, I returned to the yoke of everyday life' (*The Foreigner*). The cat which jumped onto the sofa and purred expectantly, in *The Foreigner*, when Sindi and Sheila were discussing the income tax issue has clear symbolic significance. In the same novel, June has been likened to a cat. While describing the garden of Babu's father, Sindi says : 'A thick rubber hose lay snake-like across the garden spouting water at random'. Joshi describes 'rage' powerfully in *The Last Labyrinth* : 'I felt rage whipping at the end of my spine and shooting up to the skull, to some dark hollows where the serpents slept, just waiting to be stirred'. In *The Foreigner*, Joshi uses this simile, too : 'the doubt held me by throat like a mad dog'. Monkeys, asses and donkeys have been made use of for self-criticism and as abuses and admonitions when the urge to do so is not so intense and severe :

— We didn't make an ass of ourselves (*The Foreigner*).

— You at least knew what made an ass of a man (*The Foreigner*).

— some ten-year-old American pop record braying like an ass fit to burst (*The Strange Case*).

— The girl jumped about like a monkey giggling and laughing (*The Foreigner*).

— They chattered like a bunch of post-graduate monkeys (*The Foreigner*).

We get a suggestive fish image in Joshi's *The Strange Case* : 'And you go like a fish hooked on a string, in spite of yourself'. This from the same book is a rather hackneyed one : 'I like to please as a fish likes to swim'. As for a bat image, we find this in *The Apprentice* : 'The warehouse gave the impression of perpetual dusk, the impression that a bat must have of the world'. Joshi has used a number of animals and birds etc. for this purpose. *e.g.*, jackal, mules, horse, lizard, chamelion, vulture, eagle etc. Geeta, in *The Last Labyrinth,* 'trusts like birds fly, like fish swim' and the Kathak dancer's 'little feet' are 'like a pair of pink birds' (*The Last Labyrinth*). In *The Foreigner*, the lone unexpected fly in the air-conditioned room of Mr. Khemka perhaps represents a stranger (or a foreigner) as also ill-omen. Sindi later brushed the fly away. Dhunia, in *The Strange Case,* symbolically slaps dead a fly that harasses him. Elsewhere in the novel, Joshi has said : 'The conversation ... twisted and turned like a firefly in a garden'. He mentions butterfly several times in *The Strange Case* : 'One is pinned down there (*i.e.* Delhi), like a dead butterfly, for the next six months' and 'Her mouth ... fluttered like a crushed butterfly as she wrestled with her emotion'. The dead or crushed butterflies, in particular, catch his attention. In *The Apprentice,* he describes 'Five storeys below the crowd, white as always', as milling about 'like ants'. He presents the street, in *The Foreigner,* as 'black with men, scurrying back and forth like a million ants'. Joshi uses ant as a vehicle in *The Last Labyrinth*, too : 'Would I have appeared to him like an ant threading through a mass, knocking about, against one wall, then another? As for insects, let us mention the following :

— Between us the automatic slide projector hummed like a mischievous insect (*The Foreigner*).

— The little fellow was worse than a leech (*The Strange Case*).

— All the buses and cars and taxis and men scurrying back and forth like cockroaches (*The Last Labyrinth*).

In *The Foreigner*, the spider which lost hold of the ceiling, hit the radiator and fell on the floor, is a symbol and a running commentary on the situation.

Joshi often describes the different parts of the body and tends to compare the limbs with different things, and *vice versa*. There are several aspects of the pictures of the body as we find them in his writings. He talks of the face in *The Strange Case* : 'the whitish cliff face to the right, like the mouth of the limestone quarry'. He has described the different states of the brow under the impact of different feelings : 'a streak of worry' (*The Foreigner*) and 'Ironing the crease off the brow' (*The Strange Case*). Eyes attract him and he mentions them often in interesting ways. He tends to describe eyes the way they have been in Indian literature. As a result, his descriptions often do not have much of freshness. 'Dog-like eyes' is Joshi's favourite expression.

He compares large eyes to a variety of things. This one, however, appears stale as it is characteristically repeatedly used in our country : 'Large eyes were like a lake after a rain''. The following, however, catch our attention :

— Your eyes are like jewels when sunlight falls on them (*The Foreigner*).

He thinks even about a blind man's eye :

— The river lay forzen and glazed like a blind man's eye (*The Foreigner*).

— the darkness of the night in her eyes (*The Strange Case*).

— their (evil ones) eyes, burning like coals (*The Strange Case*).

(The eyes of the juggler in his *The Last Labyrinth* are 'coal-black')

— Through the aperture, like prisoners through a grill, the Brigadier's eyes stared at me (*The Apprentice*).

— They reminded me of the eyes of a dog who has been whipped (*The Apprentice*).

The similes and metaphors in Joshi's writings often emerge, as is natural, from the contemporary setting. The fingers of Som's mother, in *The Last Labyrinth*, were 'hard as pencils'. In *The Foreigner*, Joshi talks of examination for the purpose of comparison : 'it is just the kind of fear I used to have before taking an examination or jumping from the diving board' and 'I was like the dull school boy who always get stuck with the same unanswerable questions'. We are reminded of this picture in Narayan's *The Financial Expert* : 'he looked like an examination student who has emerged from the ordeal, sapped in every way'. The talkativeness of Mrs. Blyth (in *The Foreigner*) has been presented effectively :

— 'Honolulu', shouted Mrs. Blyth, 'like a train attendant in a children's park'.

— Mrs. Blyth went on uninterruptedly like a railway conductor.

'The randomness of existence' had led Sindi towards the target 'like a programmed missile'. The images drawn from the modern business and banking are particularly interesting and effective :

— I had already given her whatever I had and there was nothing more to give ... I tried to explain this to her once or twice but she always laughed it off, saying that I talked like a banker (*The Foreigner*).

— I felt like a bankrupt manufacturer who suddenly discovers that he has something to sell (*The Foreigner*).

— Life is not a business account losses of which can be written off against the gains (*The Foreigner*).

— The crowd, which during the afternoon had had its peaks and troughs like the fluctuations of a business people, seemed to be in a trough right now (''Gherao'').

— the only thing I could think of was to get married. It was like taking out an insurance on my normalcy (*The Strange Case*).

Often Joshi singles out mercury :

— A few yards ahead of us a large wet patch of road shone like a pit full of mercury (*The Foreigner*).

— its (stream's) water was shining like so much mercury (*The Strange Case*).

Joshi occasionally explores science a little more closely. Ullmann (1966, 83) talks of Hans Sperber's semantic law that ''if we are interested in a subject, it will provide us with analogies for the description of our other experiences''. This law seems to be working in respect of the selection of images by Joshi as many images in his fiction have been brought from areas many people are now interested in :

— Any lie, however well intended, could only be a time bomb with a fuse set for some time in the unknown future (*The Foreigner*).

— Desire rose within me like water behind a broken dam (*The Foreigner*).

— It infested the skyscrapers and over the city like a pall of infectious fall out (*The Foreigner*).

— Except for the twinkling of a few lights, darkness lay upon the city like a burden of cosmic guilt (*The Foreigner*).

Sobnis, in *The Last Labyrinth*, catapulted her ideas 'with singular ferocity, charging them with the electricity of the brain'. Later in the novel, 'time itself seemed wiped off like the spools of a computer'.

Joshi has sometimes used disease and medical imagery perhaps for an accurate conveying of the nuances of the situation. These images are exact and exciting and often appear brutal and stark :

— I feared something more worse — the abominable hands groping into my soul, ripping dry scars open and dipping old wounds (*The Foreigner*).

— I felt as if some indefatigable surgeon was cleansing up my soul with the edge of his scalpel (*The Foreigner*).

— June's memory lingered with me like an incurable ulcer (*The Foreigner*).

— Have you ever lived with a tubercular? It is living with death (*The Apprentice*).

— What then had I whored to? I dismissed the remark as the bile of a disgruntled man who had not made the grade (*The Apprentice*).

— ... this apathy, this indifference, grew. Upon me. Like a boil. Like leprosy (*The Apprentice*).

— You can't do much to stop it once you get started. It is like a disease in a way, getting worse and worse (*The Apprentice*).

— Minute by minute, the question multiplied, like a virus (*The Apprentice*).

— Mrs. Biswas, realizing that she had stepped on a sore toe, quickly retreated (*The Strange Case*).

— You will live like a leper for the rest of your life (*The Strange Case*).

— (he is) like a balm on wound (*The Strange Case*).

— Deep inside my heart, I knew, I was a leper that I needed a cure (*The Last Labyrinth)*.

The images of death and decay recur in Joshi and he has been able to communicate the sadness and melancholy of the situation with the help of these images. For example :

— His mouth was pinched as of a corpse (*The Apprentice*).

— On the floor his antique record player lay like a dead man's jaw, swallowing dust (*The Foreigner*).

June's death is a symbol of a phase of 'cultural leg' (Prasad, 1985, p. 35) Sindi encounters at Khemka's house the bronze figure of the dancing *Shiva* — "The archetypal image of the dancing *Shiva* is a product of Arun Joshi's collective unconscious, his Indian heritage. It is also a correlate to the turning phase in Arun Joshi's odyssey in his life. The protagonist is a quester incognito. This image gets a fuller dimension in the symbol of Lord Krishna that pervades the whole of *The Last Labyrinth*. The dancing Shiva is the paradox of truth; he is both destructive fury and creative force" (Prasad, 1995, p. 41).

Joshi is sensitive to 'stench' and 'smell' :

— You drag your knowledge, like a rotting carcass, through the streets of the world, filling the air with stench (*The Apprentice*).

— That was the first time I came face to face with pain ... and it seemed to permeate everything like the smell of death (*The Foreigner*).

— Now I remember him like the ugly smell picked up near an open manhole (*The Foreigner*).

— In a way it was like a smell of death (*The Foreigner*).

Joshi has presented the tender and intimate feelings of love in symbolic ways. To cite an example from *The Foreigner* : 'Babu's name always seemed to unlock some hidden portals in her consciousness'.

In *The Strange Case*, Joshi talks of dipping into the 'well of silence and learning'. Benaras, Aftab, Anuradha, their haveli, in *The Last Labyrinth*, 'all were bores, frogs stuck in their marshy wells'. 'Well', in fact, has been an iterative image in Joshi's *The Apprentice* :

— I lived in a little world, frog in the well, but even frogs in the well gather ideas of what is abroad, an idea of sun and cloud, night and day.

— Our department was not the king's court. It was only a well, but the well did reflect the sky.

— As I sat in my well and watched I felt choked, oppressed; rebellious but tied up totally in knots.

— What I knew was that an epoch, as they say, had passed, but in my well all was as before.

— But what can you expect of a frog in the well, of frustrated men sailing about in a confused society.

— that crowd sauntering back and forth, eating, laughing, quarrelling. All frogs in the well.

He explores symbolic possibilities by referring to history in interesting ways : 'My old servant had not understood the purpose of my wanderings but had remained at his post like a dutiful Casablanca' (*The Foreigner*). Som, in *The Last Labyrinth*, had taken women by surprise — 'not the surprise of a Casanova'. Certainly, ordinary events have been given the status of great significance because of the 'vehicle' used. Joshi quotes Pascal and Kierkegaard, too, in *The Last Labyrinth*. Joshi takes resort to sports imagery in this novel. He says that in Benaras nothing was straightforward and adds, 'one was always running a hurdles race'. The game of chess between Aftab Rai and Som is actually a prolonged symbolic presentation of the things in the novel and a kind of commentary on them.

Joshi uses premodification with power and gusto : 'sabre-edged wit, 'hare-brained clues', 'hare-brained tribal' (*The Strange Case*) and 'the cot-farewell stage' (*The Apprentice*). 'The young men were sucked into the turbulence' (*The Apprentice*) is an example of the use of an image-making verb and 'Babu's car pulsated like a restless giant under my feet' (*The Foreigner*) that of personification. When Babu, in *The Foreigner*, is angry with Sindi, he calls him 'a conceited little squirt'. We find 'you swine', 'the Bitch' and 'the bitch, the bitch, the bitch' in Joshi's *The Strange Case*. Aftab Rai has been referred to as 'son of a bitch' in *The Last Labyrinth*. A little later in the novel, Som shouts, 'Screw the bitch'. In fact, metaphorical abuses are interspersed throughout Joshi's writings.

When he has to describe a gathering of people he says 'the crowd in little knots', 'knots of men' (*The Strange Case*) and 'a knot of men', 'knots of pilgrims' and 'a river of bobbing heads in spate' (*The Last Labyrinth*). A concretive metaphor is a picturesque way of saying something and attributes concreteness or physical existence to an abstraction. Joshi has used concretive metaphors again and again : 'a graveyard of cars' (*The Foreigner*); 'the shoulder of a ridge', 'the protective umbrella of a conventional home', 'the rosy light of the little electric flowers', 'peg of money', 'explosion of the senses' (*The Strange Case*), 'the slow leakage of hope', 'the frantic thrashing of the great sea of indifference', 'a maze of streets', 'little adultress of the soul', 'the eye of a storm' (*The Apprentice*); 'carnival of fossils' and 'an anaemic shaft of sunlight' (*The Last Labyrinth*). 'Spitting', as Joshi uses it, often shapes into an image to emphasize one's hatred for something. In his *The Foreigner* : 'I was born an Indian and had been spat upon; had I been a European, I would have done the spitting'.

Joshi sometimes makes use of phrases and proverbs metaphorically:

— I now ran about here and there, like a cock without a head, as they say in Chattisgarh (*The Strange Case*).

— Dr. Shenoy, I am afraid, appears to be a bit of a stuffed shirt (*The Strange Case*).

'A stuffed shirt' is a pet metapahor with Joshi.

— I clutched at the straw with both hands, as they say, until, of course, the straw itself broke (*The Strange Case*).

— I arrived at the fork in my life (*The Strange Case*).

— We only remember what best grinds our axe (*The Strange Case*).

'Who would sink roots in the deserts?' (*The Apprentice*) is an example of a proverb used interrogatively. Aftab Rai introduces Som to Gargi, in *The Last Labyrinth*, as a businessman whose 'touch could turn mud into gold'. This is an interesting instance of the use of 'conversational hyperbole' : 'Their muscular bodies and white flashing teeth exuded mountains of unconsumed energy that would doubtless explode in a hundred ways before the night was done' (*The Last Labyrinth*).

It is true, however, that some of the images that he has used appear stock and trite *e.g.*, 'an ocean had opened between us and the Brigadier' (*The Apprentice*), 'it came naturally like breathing' (*The Apprentice*), 'it (the money) was the djinn in the bottle' (*The Apprentice*); 'let me blow my own trumpet' (*The Apprentice*), 'things spring up, like Jack-in-the-Box, as soon as you put down your guard, as soon as the thumb on the lid weakens' (*The Apprentice*); 'I felt a great lightening, as if someone had lifted a burden from my chest' (*The Foreigner*); 'the worker's clothes were falling off in rags and sweat poured off their backs as if they just had a shower' (*The Foreigner*); 'she was still as stone' and 'as fresh as a bride' (*The Strange Case*). Ratan's apprenticeship in shoe-shining in *The Apprentice* is a beginning and may lead to the cleansing of the layers of dirt covering his soul (Iyengar, 1985, 748). Though Joshi has handled the images competently many of them remind the reader of the usual stuff in the western fiction. Many of these images are authentic Indianisms and carry an unmistakable local colour.

REFERENCES

Ali, Ahmed, 1964. *Ocean of Night.* Orient.

Iyengar, K.S., 1985. *Indian Writing in English.* Sterling.

Joshi, Arun, 1968. *The Foreigner.* Orient.

—. 1971. *The Strange Case of Billy Biswas.* Hind.

—. 1974. *The Apprentice.* Orient.

—. 1981. *The Last Labyrinth.* Orient.

Maugham, W. Somerset, 1957. *Cakes and Ale.* Pocket Book.

Narayan, R.K., 1952. *The Financial Expert.* Indian Thought.

Prasad, H.M., 1985. *Arun Joshi.* Arnold Heinneman.

Subramanyam, Kaa Naa, 1977. *Contemporary Indian Short Stories.* Bell Books.

Ullmann, S., 1966. *Language and Style.* Oxford : Basil Blackwell.

Chapter 5

VED MEHTA'S *DELINQUENT CHACHA* : A STUDY

Delinquent Chacha is the first novel ('a brilliant first novel' — Iyengar, 1985, 515) written by Ved Mehta (born in 1934 in Lahore) and was first published in 1963. Though Mehta was educated at American schools and later at Balliol College and Harvard and now lives in New York, the novel is Indian in many ways both thematically and linguistically. P. Lal (JIWE, January 1974, 20) has however remarked, 'Mr. Mehta has been too long in the West, and his Indian perceptions, rational and intuitive, have been damaged in the process'. The English that Mehta uses in the novel shows his mastery over the language. The language, however, is often very stiff and formal. Mehta has frequently resorted to esoteric vocabulary, long and convoluted sentences and paragraphs. He has been mentioned as a member of the so-called 'unholy triumvirate' (Kumar, 1987) – Nirad Chaudhuri and V.S. Naipaul are the other members. It has been said that these writers have been constantly mimicking their western masters in their style and attitude.

Delinquent Chacha finds himself at a loss to see that Englishmen have left India. He has a 'nostalgia for the lost empire', wants to turn himself into an Englishman and has a great desire to have 'the advantage of a chivalrous association with the British' (48). He goes to the extent of saying : 'India ... on which the sun permanently set the day the British left' (26) and talks of 'the innate superiority' of Britons (64). He held the hand of the narrator 'in a firm, powerful grip, like an Englishman' (24) and 'had a lifelong ambition to pass for a gentleman' (25). Delinquent Chacha eagerly looks forward to his going home when he will be known as "England-returned" and when he will instruct his grandchildren 'in the ways of the British' (41). As Iyengar (1985, 517) observes, 'the novel is a satire on Indians who have madly gone foreign'.

In Delinquent Chacha, Mehta has in fact created 'a large scale comic character'. He is the central character of the novel and the novel is wholly about him. He talks in an elegant but affected manner. Wit and humour are the essential and integral features of Ved Mehta's style in the book ('pure — almost transcendent fun' — Iyengar, 1985, 515). Whatever Delinquent Chacha says and whatever has been said about him are more or less, as a rule, humorous, sometimes ridiculous. Delinquent Chacha has been referred to as 'the greatest failure in the memory' of the narrator's family (9) and his career as 'a long and successful career as a poor relation' (10). Kaka, the narrator, received at Oxford the letter sent by Delinquent Chacha from Suez. As the letter was a mixture of Urdu and English, 'with sometimes a line changing direction half way', just to glance at a page was to have 'a sensation of seasickness' (25). Chacha had to walk around the streets for nearly two hours to shake the smell of camphor out of his clothes (30). Mr. Hartwell addresses him as 'Delinquent' and asks him 'do you mind if I call you by your Christian name' (30). Chacha wants to pull a couple of tables together and catch forty winks (39). When Delinquent Chacha tells the African that his hobby since boyhood has been rearing cub lions and tigers and baby elephants (the repeated use of the conjunction 'and' is interesting and reminds us of Raja Rao) the narrator interrupts to add — 'Delinquent Chacha had never set eyes on a jungle animal except in the zoo' (47). When Chacha wears the British suit, he speaks disparagingly of the Indian pyjama cord — 'It leaves marks around the waist, and your Delinquent Chacha has found breathing God's good air difficult because of the constriction of the diaphragm' (48). When a rather beefy man with a long English face and tousled hair walked into the room, Chacha started bragging about himself and interrupted his speech by uttering asides like 'Do you think that Brussels sprout of an Englishman is taking all this in' (52). In the Model United Nations session the Pakistan Chairman reports that their delegation had already drafted a resolution which would force the Indian government to give back the holy place (the Taj Mahal!) to its rightful and true owners (*i.e.* Pakistan) and arrange for a safe access to it through a special corridor. In his letter to the Queen Elizabeth II, Delinquent Chacha compares the pandemonium at the mock United Nations to the Sepoy Mutiny — he requests the Queen to make him a Knight of the Order of the Garter ("C.M.G. is not enough") in a hurry, so that he can help ride out the storm (126). While in the dock, Chacha turns around and calls his nephew, the narrator, 'Kaka, come!' to testify that he had a bent towards philosophy all his life (101). When the court objects to it he asks, 'May I, then not summon my Kaka?'. When he is happy with his counsel he shouts from the dock itself, 'Hear! hear! Good show, McLean!' for which he is admonished by the bench (104). When he is not happy with his counsel he wants to relieve him of his 'burdensome' duties and argue his case himself and adds, 'McLean, my dear fellow, no hard feelings —' (114). The novel is interspersed with this kind of pure, broad, innocent humour — all this makes it a thoroughly readable stuff.

Delinquent Chacha has been likened to Dickens' well-known character, Micawber. When we are told that Delinquent Chacha 'has ever been banking on luck turning' (28) we are at once reminded of Micawber. Without mentioning Micawber directly, the judge, while giving judgment in favour of Delinquent Chacha, says, '... it could be that, like a certain famous character in fiction, he was confidently, although perhaps over-optimistically, waiting for "something to turn up" which would enable him to meet his commitments' (124). Delinquent Chacha may also be fruitfully compared with some of R.K. Narayan's characters particularly with Margayya of *The Financial Expert* and Mr. Sampath. Both Delinquent Chacha and Margayya appear innocent in all their crookedness. Delinquent Chacha has 'a vivid fantasy life' (97).

Though Ved Mehta virtually migrated to England at a relatively raw age the language he uses in the novel is not without Indianisms — the expressions with Indian flavour which remind us of their oft-used equivalents in Indian languages. Delinquent Chacha tells the boy in the coffee house, 'if he allows anyone up here I'll cut his throat' (11). The contracted verbal form 'I'll' deserves a mention here as the use of this nature is a distinctive feature of conversation. Delinquent Chacha tells Kaka — 'Your Delinquent Chacha, unless he wishes to cut his nose in the family, has to put in an appearance' (42). Later he says to Mr. Stubbs of 'the School and University Outfitters' — 'The bills simply waited until the young man found his feet — got established in society' (70). Delinquent Chacha tells the court, 'if we get nine customers a day we count ourselves lucky' (112) and that 'they (the young barristers) still have their name to make' (112). Lala Suraj Pal, the owner of the All India Taj Mahal Curry, Chutney, and Soup Restaurant where Delinquent Chacha was employed, tells the court, 'Ram is my witness' (193) and later talks of Karma, Dharma and Maya all in a single statement before the court.

Mehta has apparently not cared for proportions. The size of dialogues and sentences is often unnaturally and inexplicably long. For example, when Kaka asks Delinquent Chacha as to why S.S.S. Singh left Punjab to go away to the foreign south the reply given by Chacha runs uninterruptedly into some 115 lines (17-21). Delinquent Chacha's letter which he sent to Kaka from Suez runs into some 9 pages though it ends abruptly and has not been reproduced fully (26-34). The novel ends with another letter written by Delinquent Chacha, this time to the Queen Elizabeth II of Britain which runs into 2 pages. The narrator in fact concedes that it was characteristic of Delinquent Chacha to indulge himself in rhetoric instead of instantly explaining the main issue (26). In the letter written from Suez he is reminded of the old New Delhi Coffee House where they had eaten before the narrator left for Oxford and, thereafter, tells Kaka that he 'wouldn't recognize the place now' and goes on to give the details with regard to the changes that have occurred at the Coffee House. The letter, therefore, is rambling in nature and may perhaps be considered as an instance of 'stream of consciousness'.

In his letters Delinquent Chacha again and again gives the impression as if he was addressing or delivering a speech. He talks of 'the vicinity of the Coffee House' and hurriedly adds, 'It maintains its old name' and then completes the sentence. He informs Kaka how he told Mr. Hartwell that his brothers were very well-placed 'and my nephew — you, Kaka — is at Oxford'. In fact, this variety of interrupted sentences, a feature usually associated with conversation, has been often made use of by Mehta in the novel. There is a very big interruption in the middle of a sentence when the counsel for the prosecution makes his opening statement (96) whereas this one is a case of interruption in the form of a question — 'if the answers to these questions be in the affirmative — and can you have any doubts? — then you should have no hesitation in declaring the accused guilty and putting him behind bars' (100). At the same time, there are short, minor, grammatically incomplete sentences — characteristic of informal language — like 'More laughter' (96).

The letter that Delinquent Chacha wrote to Kaka after the Model United Nations row at Oxford has been written on a telegram blank and in the style of a telegram :

ONE WORD IN OBSERVER BETTER THAN HUNDRED IN TIMES OF INDIA OR NEW YORK TIMES STOP HARK EXCLAMATION... AM PUZZLED STOP .... OH COMMA NO WORD OR TRIAL SHOULD REACH EARS OF FAMILY FOR THEIR BASIC LACK OF KNOWLEDGE OF WORLD WILL LEAD TO UNNECESSARY WORRY STOP

On the back there was hasty scribbling — 'Oh, that your Delinquent Chacha were so well-heeled that this important communique could be urgently dispatched by means of Morse Code — da-da, da-da'. The point which should be borne in mind here is that the reference in *Observer* was a report of Chacha's prosecution.

Though it has been said about Mehta that he is 'more international than Indian' (Williams, 1976, 103), his language in the novel is not without occasional cliche — the expressions which have lost freshness due to overuse and which a writer should, as far as possible, avoid and instead prefer a new and original one. Delinquent Chacha tries to use a certain kind of flowery language all the time though he has not received much of formal education. That is why it is but natural for him to use expressions which, at first sight, look like cliches. Some of the cliche-like expressions used in the novel are heart-to-heart (9), beck and call (10), as our good fortune would have it (17), with aplomb (46), needless to say (98), need I add (99), to tell the truth (110) and make heads and tails (110). Mehta makes a serious attempt to describe the voice vividly — 'cathedral voice', 'gheelike voice' and 'oily voice'. Incidentally, 'the oily voice' has been a favourite with Indian writers in English.

Though not very often, he makes use of similes and metaphors in the novel. Delinquent Chacha finds the American gentleman 'fresh as the morning dew' (28) and he 'was gripped with fear that Hartwell would slip out of my fingers like myna' (31). The President of the model United Nations at Oxford remarks, 'my ears were clean as a police whistle' (75). The Pakistani delegate calls Delinquent Chacha a veritable cobra 'we have allowed ... to nestle in our bosom' (85) and asserts that 'no political question can be settled, however small — let alone the biggest of them all, the question of the ownership of the Taj Mahal — until we seize this serpent, squash its head, and pluck it out'. In fact, it is an extended metaphor and has been carried forward and the whole of the next paragraph has to do with it. The Indian colloquial conversation, as we know, is often replete with the references to cobras, serpents and the like. We find in the novel some sad pictures — the objective correlative, to be exact. The Royal Colonial Club was funereal and dark (45). Lala Suraj Pal appears in the court in 'funereal black' (100). For some time, Kaka, Chacha and the African sat in a tomb-like silence (46). Mehta makes metaphoric use of the vivid verbs — image-making verbs with connotative power :

— 'off with you, off with you', he said, propelling me toward the door (43).

— I had wedged it (the Indian pan) into my mouth (43).

— ambled out of the room (103).

As is apparent, many images here are perhaps not very fresh and original ones. Maybe people will find some of them 'dead' or 'half-dead'.

Ved Mehta's style is well-studded with old-fashioned and archaic expressions some of which appear unnatural and out of place. Instead of 'letter' he has used 'epistle' (23), in the place of 'dress' he prefers 'attire' (9) and 'adornment' (118) and instead of 'ages' he uses 'aeons' (99). This kind of use often adds a tinge of formality to the language in which they occur. Now and then, Mehta has used rare and unusual words and expressions (*e.g.*, 'contrapuntal epiphany' and 'whippersnapper' etc.) though one of the most easily noticeable aspects of informal language is its vocabulary which tends to be very simple. Lala Suraj Pal uses in the court a non-specific prop word 'you-know-whats' which functions as a noun. Interestingly, Mehta has a peculiar fascination for French words and often makes his characters utter them e.g., *entre nous* (47), *avant garde* (55) and *objets d'art* (56) etc. Mehta has frequently italicized words, phrases and sentences in order to place stress. This has been done more often in the chapter dealing with court proceedings.

Mehta often makes use of certain anaphoric features of language *e.g.*, the substitute word 'one'. Though the use of the preposition at the end is absolutely acceptable now its actual occurrence in speech is generally sparing and not so common. However, prepositions are often placed towards the end in Mehta's sentences and expressions *e.g.*, 'I haven't told you the main thing I arranged this meeting for' (22), 'you are the person I thought of writing to first' (23), 'I used to tell you stories about' (26), 'as splendid a peg ... as the Royal Colonial Club of the British Empire to hang my hat on' (47), 'Kaka, imagine, if you are able to' (56) and 'to benefit therefrom' (78). Sometimes such a use is accompanied with inversion — 'Divorce there could be no question of' (56).

An interesting aspect of the Indian speech habit, as we know, is that again and again there are numerical assertions — 'lexical' as well as 'conversational' hyperbole, so to say. They are employed particularly for emphasis and to give the writing a more intimate local colour. Mehta makes good use of it : 'Oh, Lala! Oh, Lala! ... May God give you a thousand tongues and a thousand liberal hands' (40). True, the kind of character that Delinquent Chacha is, it is but natural that he will speak in this vein.

Towards the end of the novel (92-124) a large chunk has to do with the hearing in the court of law of Delinquent Chacha's case — he was charged with fraudulently obtaining clothes and credit. A number of things in this section are apparently variety-specific, the legal language. The linguistic conservatism of legal English, the chain-like nature of some of the constructions, the presence of Latin phrases *'ipso facto'* and *'mutatis mutandis'* and of legal cliche *e.g.*, 'remiss', 'summation' and 'rested' etc. catch our attention in the text. Ved Mehta has made an authentic use of the vocabulary of the law. Synonymous or near-synonymous phrases have been occasionally coordinated, as is often done in legal English.

The language, as a whole, is slightly removed from 'informal spontaneous conversation' (Crystal and Davy, 1969, 194). The novel has been acclaimed as a first-rate farce. The tone is certainly light. Though the situation is important the story moves round a single character. Quite a few things in the novel give a mock appearance, the look of caricature, and the novel is crowded with witty as well as foolish remarks, humorous passages and hilariously funny situations. The dilemma before Delinquent Chacha is that of reconciling east-west values. It is difficult for him to get past the colonial experience and free himself from the western attraction. Perhaps Delinquent Chacha is a caricature of people who were 'queer mixture of the East and West, out of place everywhere, at home nowhere', 'a fairly typical figure in Indian society' (Iyengar, 1985, 515).

REFERENCES

Crystal D. and Davy D., 1969. *Investigating English Style*. Longman.

Iyengar, K.R.S., 1985 edition. *Indian Writing in English*, New Delhi : Sterling.

Kumar, Shiv K., Of 'mimic men'. In *The Hindustan Times, Sunday Magazine*, February 15, '87.

Mehta, Ved, 1969. *Delinquent Chacha*. London : Collins (all references to this edition).

Williams, H.M., 1976. *Indo-Anglian Literature 1800-1970 : A Survey*. Madras: Orient Longman.

Chapter 6

WHEN ALL'S SAID AND DONE ...
The Cliche and Indo-English Fiction

C.P. Snow coined the phrase 'corridors of power' in his novel *Home Comings.* In the author's note to his novel which he interestingly named *Corridors of Power,* Snow tells us that the catchy phrase was picked up and used by journalists and reviewers so many times that it turned into a cliche. When Snow was charged with using a cliche for a title, he retorted, 'if a man hasn't the right to his own cliche, who has?' Snow's consolation was that at least he had used his own cliche. A cliche is 'a hackneyed phrase or expression which a writer keeps ready stock set up in his mind and puts down automatically without troubling to find an original phrase of his own' (Wood, 1962, 47). The fact, however, remains that the phrases of this nature, as Wood, too, has emphasized, 'should, as far as possible, be avoided' as 'at one time they may have been forceful; now they are stale and ineffective'. Vallins (1960,103) talks of 'the sterile lifelessness of a cliche'.

What needs to be added here is that even native writers of English have not been able to avoid cliche altogether. This, for example, is a sentence from W. Somerset Maugham's novel *Cakes and Ale* (p. 24) : 'when all's said and done, that's the only thing that counts'. The phrase has been used by Mulk Raj Anand in *Two Leaves and a Bud* (p. 91), by Khushwant Singh in *Train to Pakistan*; by Arun Joshi in *The Strange Case of Billy Biswas* (p.50), *The Apprentice* (p. 80), and *The Last Labyrinth* (p. 202, p. 203) and by Uma Vasudev in *The Song of Anasuya* (p.71). There is little doubt that it is not possible to shun the cliche completely. They come handy and readily to a writer and, as many believe, sometimes add flavour to writing. Crystal and Davy think that the occasional cliche is a feature of the informality of a text (1969,114). Fowler (1968,9) feels that writers would be needlessly handicapped if they were never allowed to choose certain expression — they are perhaps the fittest way of saying what needs to be said. Fowler quotes J.A. Spender : 'The hardest worked cliche is better than the phrase that fails'.

When Sheila says, in Arun Joshi's *The Foreigner* (p.149), 'Time is a great healer', Sindi argues — 'However deeply one might feel, it always boils down to a cliche, a proverb from high school grammar'. Joshi apparently confuses between a cliche and a proverb. A cliche can usually be traced to a definite author while the latter is just as often anonymous (Pei, 1953, 144). Undoubtedly, however, many proverbs, due to gross overuse, have turned into cliches and in this study we do not intend to make any sharp distinction between them. It should also be borne in mind, at the same time, that the judgement whether a certain expression is a cliche or not is often a subjective one. While analysing R.K. Narayan's "A House and Two Goats", Rao (1978) quotes the phrase "live, flourish and die" and says it 'is not as much of a cliche as it appears; there is an unsuspected, seemingly endless agony between *flourish* and *die*'. Pei (1953, 143) notes that the ancestry of the cliche 'is nine times out of ten literary, even though it may have entered the universal spoken language'. Chaucer, Shakespeare, Milton, Keats and Kipling etc., for example, have been fruitful sources of cliches for the English speaking world.

The point that I would like to make in this study is that Indian writers in English sometimes do not exert to find a novel or original phrase. Instead they prefer to make do with some prefabricated or conventional overused 'pat' expression. Singh (1977,185) finds it not unusual to come across cliches in their writings. One possible explanation and the one that we would like to make forcefully here is that the presence of these cliches in their writings can be explained, to some extent, when we bear in mind the fact that English is not their first language. When we adopt L_2 or a foreign language at the creative level we are perhaps more prone to confront such difficulties as we are often bookish and our vocabulary is anything but vast though, to assert once again, even the native speakers are faced with these obstacles. In fact, 'some commentators on Indian English have noticed an excessive use of cliche' (McCrum, Cran, MacNeil, 1986). Chitre (1978) observes that 'diseased English' (quick-frozen, ready to use English) is normal English in India and the official English, very widely used in India, is the deadliest form of diseased English. Nambiar (1978) also stresses that a characteristic feature of Indian English, as presented by earlier British writers, is the presence of cliches. When Nergis Dalal (1978) reviews Pramill Bharat Singh's *The*

Reluctant Bride (Sterling) she finds it full of cliches (*Times of India*, October 22 1978).

I would like to make my point particularly with the help of illustrations borrowed from the representative fictional writings of Indian writers in English (on the basis of random sampling).

Though Raja Rao's writings are relatively free from cliches we occasionally do get instances like 'to tell you the truth' (*Kanthapura*, p. 20). One comes across 'to tell the truth' in Ved Mehta's *Delinquent Chacha* (p. 110), Joshi's *The Strange Case* (p. 132), Uma Vasudev's *The Song of Anasuya* (p.3) and Salman Rushdie's *Midnight's Children* (p.114, 301). Mulk Raj Anand's writings are interspersed with cliche-like expressions *e.g.*, the conventional phrase 'wonder of all wonders' (*Coolie*, p. 31) and phrases 'going to the dogs' (*Coolie*, p. 126); also in R.K. Narayan's *The Guide*, (p. 180) and 'he had missed the bus' (*Coolie*, p. 126), 'waxing philosophical' (*Two Leaves and a Bud*, p. 18); 'waxed eloquent' in Narayan's *The Guide* (p. 154), and 'wax poetic' in Joshi's *The Strange Case*, 'he felt like a fish out of water' (*Two Leaves and a Bud*, p. 26), 'at a standstill' (*Two Leaves*, p. 29), 'discretion is the better part of valour' (*Death of a Hero*, Anand, p. 13), 'under the thumb of his father' (*Death of a Hero*, p. 59), 'hitch our wagon to the Maharaja's fading star' (*Death of a Hero*, p. 74); also in *My God Died Young*, Sasthi Brata, p. 147). Anand evidently uses various kinds of cliche. Cowasjee (1976, p. 59) quotes a passage from Anand's *Two Leaves* and concludes that the passage is full of well-worn cliches.

The same goes for R.K. Narayan whose favourite phrase is the Siamese twin 'odds and ends' (*Swami and Friends*, p. 32, 195; *The Vendor of Sweets*, pp. 25, 119, 158). 'Odds and ends' appears to be Joshi's pet expression, too, because he has used it both in *The Foreigner* (p. 162) and *The Strange Case* (p. 62). 'Odds and ends' has also been used by Abbas in *Maria* (p. 47) and by Namita Gokhahe in *Gods, Graves and Grandmother* (p. 53). Gokhale has used 'to no avail' again and again (pp. 34, 36). Talking of Narayan's *Swami and Friends*, it has 'by any chance' (p.44), 'the servant beat a hasty retreat' (p.44), 'drove home the point' (p. 51), 'half a mind' (p. 88), 'Right O' (p. 90), 'more easily said than done' (p.129), also in *The Strange Case*, (Joshi, p. 65), 'stereotyped question' (p.169) and 'he is a gem' (p.173). *Swami and Friends* is Narayan's first full-length work of fiction and that perhaps explains why it contains a fair sprinkling of cliches. Of the 'big three', Narayan perhaps uses more of such expressions and some of them have been used again and again. One of the possible reasons may be that simplicity is the hallmark of Narayan's style. The following are some more examples from Narayan's works :

'To make a clean breast of it all' (p.109), 'like a bolt from the blue' (p.147), 'cleared out' (p. 205) and 'bag and baggage' (p.205) : *The Guide.* 'Cleared out' and 'bag and baggage' have been used again in his *The Bachelor of Arts* (p.117). 'A fault-finding mood' (p.22), 'a stone's throw' (p.29), 'where there was a will there was a way' (p.112) and 'out of sight out of mind' (p.144) — *The Bachelor of Arts.*

'thus far and no further' (p.144) and 'for reasons best known to them' (p.153); also in *The Song of Anasuya*, Uma Vasudev, (p. 35) : *A Tiger for Malgudi.* 'Best chum' (p.6), 'ravages of time' and 'a whit lost' (p. 42) : *My Days.* 'Stick to the point' (p. 27), 'it goes without saying' (p. 61), 'go straight to the point' (p.139), 'you have beaten about the bush' (p. 139), 'unheard of' (p.143), 'go to hell' (p.147) and 'from time immemorial' (p. 164) — *The Vendor of Sweets.* 'A serious blunder' (p. 57): *The English Teacher.*

These are from Malgonkar's books :

'rank and file of the spectators' (p. 9), 'the stormy petrol' (p. 36), 'putting the clock back' (p. 89), 'all told' (p. 125), 'beaten them to pulp' (p. 178) and 'paled into significance' (p. 267) — *A Bend in the Ganges.*

'at breakneck speed' (p.16), 'made good his escape' (p. 365), 'call it a day' (p.111) — *Spy in Amber.*

Kamala Markandaya

''in the twinkling of an eye' (p. 25), 'next to impossible' (p.180) — *Nectar in a Sieve.*

'umpteen babies' (p. 49), 'umpteen servants' (p.200), 'all and sundry' (p.45), 'at her wit's end' (p.76), 'cat'll be out of the bag' (p.208), 'she felt she was on fire' (p.218), 'cry over spilt milk' (p.233) and 'at the end of the tether' — *Two Virgins*; 'near the end of the tether' in Joshi's *The Strange Case*; 'needless to say' (pp. 1, 14, 21, 43), 'born and brought up' (p. 15), 'few loose ends still to be tied' (p. 20) and 'out of the question' (p. 21) — *Possession.*

A possible explanation as to why Raja Rao and Markandaya (though 'needless to say' is her pet expression) use fewer stock phrases and formulae may be that both of them have been away from India for long.

Arun Joshi's writings

'for no accountable reason' (p. 25), 'much aplomb' (p. 36), 'some big shot' (p. 40), 'to do the needful' (pp. 65, 146), 'the long and the short of the story' (p. 66), 'wag your tongue' (p. 114), 'dirty linen' (p. 79), 'head over heels' (p. 91), 'gone haywire' (p. 92), 'cooked up this cock and bull story' (p. 204) — *The Strange Case of Billy Biswas.*

'in no uncertain terms' (p.25), 'talk of the town' (p.31), 'something is better than nothing' (p. 42), 'to cut a long story short' (pp. 60, 107), 'the pros and cons of a case' (p. 65), 'in a nutshell' (p. 68), 'axe to grind' (p. 71), 'out of the ordinary' (p. 110), 'by hook or by crook' (p. 113) – an instance of Siamese twin, 'rise to the occasion' (p. 117), 'in due course' (p. 118) — *The Apprentice*, 'pain in the neck' (p. 113) — *The Last Labyrinth*.

In Anita Desai's books we get uses of this type only few and far between. In her *Voices in the City*, however, we get 'ivory tower' (p. 201) and 'lull before storm' (p. 226) etc. Bhabani Bhattacharya has used 'played his cards well' (p. 28), 'article of faith' (p. 29), 'first things first' (p.34), 'like a bombshell' (p. 34) and 'life is a game of cards' (p.79), in his *So Many Hungers!* and 'the less said the better' (p.39) in *Shadow From Ladakh*. In addition to a number of items of this nature, Khushwant Singh's *Train to Pakistan* carries 'crystal clear' and his *I Shall Not Hear the Nightingale* 'who is to bell the cat' (p. 27). Ahmed Ali's *Ocean of Night* carries 'build castles in the air' (p. 123). Santha Rama Rau's *The Adventuress* has 'I'll keep my fingers crossed' (p. 74) and 'in love and war, all's fair' (p. 168) and Sasthi Brata's *My God Died Young* 'they 'll hit the bull's eye'. We find 'facts and figures' (p. 68), 'took it for granted' (p. 69), 'classical joke' (p.74) and 'like deadwood' in Nayantara Sahgal's *Storm in Chandigarh* and 'best possible investments' (p. 98) and 'throwing money down the drain' (p. 98) in Saros Cowasjee's *Goodbye to Elsa*. 'Suffice it to say' (p. 35) and 'out of the blue' (p.141) in Uma Vasudev's *The Song of Anasuya,* 'as luck would have it' (*My Story*, Kamala Das, p. 82), 'nobodies' (*The Girls from Overseas,* Nergis Dalal, p. 24), 'more often than not' (*Beyond Punjab*, Prakash Tandon, p. 71), 'irregular hours' (p. 124) and 'to top it all' in "The Mixed Metaphor" (in Keki Daruwala's *Sword and Abyss*) are some more interesting examples from these writings. It may not be out of place to mention here that Chinua Achebe has used 'as luck would have it' twice in his short story "Uncle Ben's Choice".

Many similes found in these writings are indeed 'mere cliches with very little life in them' (*Vallins,* 1960, 44) *e.g.*, 'she is like a sister to me' (*The Guide*, Narayan, p. 78), 'you are as a sister to me' (*Kanthapura*, Raja Rao, p. 37), 'she was still as stone' (*The Strange Case,* Joshi, p. 62), 'the cool words hit him like a blow' (p. 5), 'he was impetuous, like a boy' (p. 91) and 'for some time he would live like a king' (p.161) in Bhattacharya's *So Many Hungers*! 'his fingers were like ice' (p. 373), 'I am going to stick here like a glue' (p. 350), 'money was spent like water' (p. 51) in Malgonkar's *A Bend in the Ganges* and 'the room is an oven' in Desai's *Voices*. The devotees in Narayan's *The Guide* held Raju 'as if he was a baby'. The touch of the hand was likened to a flame in Markandaya's *Two Virgins* and Malgonkar's *A Bend in the Ganges*. The so-called 'stabilizers' like 'as a matter of fact' (*The Strange Case*, p. 73) are not uncommon either. It goes without saying that they appear stock and trite and are in use on a large scale and often indiscriminately in India and generally have a first-to-hand quality about them. Perhaps they help the writers present the goings-on a little more realistically and spontaneously.

Wood (1962, 47) has roughly classified the cliche into seven broad divisions. It is interesting to note that we get examples of all these types in the Indian writing in English :

(i) *Conventional phrases or expressions* :

'the evening of the life' (*Storm in Chandigarh*, p. 5)

'by leaps and bounds' (*Storm in Chandigarh*, p. 61)

'wheel of time' (*Death of a Hero*, Anand, p. 26)

'jaws of death' (*Death of a Hero*, p. 84)

'for all practical purposes' (*Maria*, Abbas, p. 45).

(ii) *The Conventional Adjective* :

'Golden promises' (*Two Leaves and a Bud*, Anand, p. 6).

(iii) *The Conventional Verb* :

'the engine screamed' (*Coolie*, p.174); 'he shepherded them' (*Storm in Chandigarh*, p.47); 'the sentry barked' (*A Bend in the Ganges*, p. 182). The humanizing use of the verbs 'hissing' and 'stabbing' seems to be very common with them.

(iv) *The Conventional Adverb* :

'The fire was blazing fiercely' (*Nectar in a Sieve*, p. 56). 'Sheepishly' is in very coomon use in these writings.

(v) *Circumlocution* :

'the edge of her tongue was like a pair of scissors' (*i.e.* 'Talkative') — (*Untouchable*, Anand)

'We have only a loin-cloth width of land' (*Kanthapura*, Raja Rao, p. 179)

(vi) *Vogue Words* :

'movie' — 'a Bergman movie' (*The Strange Case*, p.95); 'fellow-travellers' (*A Bend in the Ganges,* p. 355); 'jet' — 'jet of water' (*Ocean of Night*, p. 62), 'jets of white stream' (*Voices,* p.5); 'electricity' — 'electric current' (*Ocean of Night*, p.46), 'electric shock' (*Maria*, Abbas, p.43); 'Valve' is another vogue word to be found in these writings again and again.

(vii) *Hackneyed and Pointless Similes* :

— 'My old servant had not understood the purpose of my wanderings but had remained at his post like a dutiful Casablanca' (*The Foreigner*, Joshi, p.352)

— 'They were all staring at him, making him conscious of their fear and hatred, like characters in some dance drama' (*A Bend in the Ganges,* p.132)

— 'They just gazed at me, as I have noticed Indian village urchins gazing at a passing elephant in our villages' ("Bosanski Novi", Kaa Naa Subramanyam).

Evidently, Indian writers in English have not been very successful in avoiding these hardened set phrases or cliches. Ullmann (1966, p.166) would like the writers to rejuvenate the set expressions and infuse new life into them. It would be perhaps not a tall claim that now and then our writers have been able to do so. It is satisfying to note that in these writings cliches on the surface do not always reflect deeper cliches of thought. The sincerity of most of them can hardly be doubted. Maybe the oral tradition and the actual speech habits, often replete with cliches, get reflected. The learners of English in India are taught during the formative period, idioms, phrases and sayings etc. so seriously and diligently that they often become an integral and essential part of their linguistic repertoire and keep making appearances in their speech and writing.

Our writers have made attempts, often unconsciously, to remedy the situation, at least to some extent, by taking resort to Indianisms. With some reservations, we approve of many of them though, in any case, they should not be overdone. Some of the verbs and phrases introduced by Mulk Raj Anand, for example, are perhaps instances of over-doing. If the writers go on taking liberties with the language in this manner the result may be ridiculous. Instead of saying 'nip it in the bud', Raja Rao, in a characteristically Indian way, has said 'crush in the seed'. Money has been frequently used for comparisons. Also, there are often hyperbolic numerical assertions — 'The saying is worth a hundred thousand rupees' (*Train to Pakistan*, Khushwant Singh). Let us cite a few more examples from Indian fiction in English :

- As long as he is there no one can harm a single hair of my head.
- Where does your wealth reside, Babu Sahib? My poor home is in Jhelum district.
- Does my lap bite you?
- No one can stop anyone's mouth.
- Have you not mother or sister in your home?
- drinking water out of the same pitcher.
- Don't eat my head.
- bread of illegality.
- your good name.

REFERENCES

Ali, Ahmed. *Ocean of Night* (Delhi : Orient Paperback, 1964).

Anand, Mulk Raj. *Coolie* (Delhi : Orient Paperback, 1972).

——. *Death of a Hero* (Delhi : Orient Paperback).

——. *Two Leaves and a Bud* (Delhi : Mayfair Paperback, 1981).

Bhattacharya, Bhabani. *So Many Hungers!* (Delhi : Orient Paperback, 1978).

——. *Shadow From Ladakh* (Delhi : Orient Paperback, 1966).

Brata, Sasthi. *My God Died Young* (Delhi : Orient Paperback, 1967).

Chitre, Dilip. 1978. Bonsai English. *The Times of India*, November 19.

Cowasjee, Saros. 1976. *Coolie* : An Assessment (Delhi : OUP).

Crystal, D. & Davy, D. *Investigating English Style* (Longman : 1969).

Dalal, Nergis. *The Girls from Overseas* (Delhi : Hind, 1979).

Daruwala, Keki. *Sword and Abyss* (Delhi : Bell Books, 1979).

Das, Kamala. *My Story* (Delhi : Sterling Paperback, 1976).

Desai, Anita. *Voices in the City* (Delhi : Orient Paperback, 1965).

Fowler, H.W. *A Dictionary of Modern English Usage* (ELBS & OUB, 1968).

Gokhale, Namita. *Gods, Graves and Grandmother* (Delhi : Rupa, 1994).

Joshi, Arun. *The Foreigner* (Delhi : Orient Paperback, 1968).

——. *The Strange Case of Billy Biswas* (Delhi : Orient Paperback, 1971).

——. *The Apprentice.* (Delhi : Orient Paperback, 1977).

——. *The Last Labyrinth* (Delhi : Orient Paperback, 1981).

Leech, G.N. *A Linguistic Guide to English Poetry.* (Longmans, 1969).

Malgonkar, Manohar. *A Bend in the Ganges* (Delhi : Orient Paperback, 1962).

——. *The Princes* (Delhi : Orient Paperback).

——. *Spy in Amber* (Delhi : Orient Paperback).

Markandaya, Kamala. *Nectar in a Sieve* (Bombay : Jaico, 1955).

Markandaya, Kamala. *Possession* (Bombay : Jaico, 1963).

——. *Two Virgins* (Delhi : Tarang Paperback, 1973).

Maugham, W.S. *Cakes and Ale* (New York : Pocket Books, INC, 1957).

McCrum, R., Cran. W. & MacNeil, R. *The Story of English* (Delhi : OUP, 1986).

Mehta, Ved. *Delinquent Chacha* (London : Collins, 1969).

Nambiar, K.C. 1978. The Language of the Indo-Anglian Novelist. In : *Indian Writing in English*. Edit. Ramesh Mohan (Madras : Orient Longman).

Narayan, R.K. *The Guide* (Mysore : Indian Thought, 1958).

——. *The Bachelor of Arts* (Mysore : Indian Thought, 1965).

——. *The Vendor of Sweets* (Mysore : Indian Thought, 1967).

——. *Swami and Friends* (Mysore : Indian Thought, 1971 reprint).

——. *The English Teacher* (Mysore : Indian Thought, 1955).

——. *My Days* (Mysore : Indian Thought, 1975).

——. *A Tiger for Malgudi* (Mysore : Indian Thought, 1984).

Pei, Mario. *The Story of English* (London : George Allen & Unwin, 1953).

Rao, Raja. *Kanthapura* (Delhi : Orient Paperback).

Rao, V.P., 1978. The Craftsmanship of R.K. Narayan. In *Indian Writing in English*. Edit. Ramesh Mohan (Madras : Orient Longman).

Rushdie, Salman. *Midnight's Children* (New York : Avon Books, 1980).

Singh, Khushwant. *I Shall Not Hear the Nightingale* (Bombay : IBH, 1970).

——. *Train to Pakistan* (Bombay : IBH, 1975).

Singh, R.S. *Indian Novel in English* (New Delhi : Arnold Heinemann, 1977).

Subramanyam, Kaa Naa. *Contemporary Indian Short Stories*. (Bell Books, 1977).

Ullmann, Stephen. *Language and Style.* (Oxford : Basil Blackwell, 1966).

Vallins, G.H. *The Best English* (ELBS, 1971).

Vasudev, Uma. *The Song of Anasuya* (Delhi : Vikas, 1978).

Wood, F.T. *Current English Usage* (London : ELBS & Macmillan, 1962).

Chapter 7

AN ASPECT OF THE IMPACT OF ENGLISH ON URDU

One of the ways in which a language changes is when it incorporates into its vocabulary and syntax, etc., uses, expressions and patterns translated into it from other languages. It is true, however, that this type of change has not always been adequately studied. It is also true, at the same time, that in some cases of this nature a certain amount of disagreement exists among the scholars of the so-called recipient language about the source of the new expression. What we plan to do here is that we will take into consideration certain expressions in use now in Urdu which appear to be literally translated from English. It should be conceded, however, that many new uses fade away as quickly as they appear; some are used only in colloquialism, some graduate to the literary language and eventually find a place in the vocabulary. When we come across such an expression we cannot often help feeling that it is a literal translation from another language — we are reminded about the equivalent expression in the other or source language. Gyan Chand (1986 : 8) points out that a bogus piece of writing which was claimed to be very old was found not that old because of the use in it of the expression 'maadri zabaan' which, as Gyan Chand says, is a literal translation of the English 'Mother Tongue' and, therefore, cannot be that old. At a place, the famous Urdu short story writer, Saadat Hasan Manto has written — 'maeN jab wahaaN se UTThaa to eik khush aadmii nahiN thaa' — when I left that place I was not a happy man — and he added thereafter that though the sentence betrayed Englishness he liked it. Six of 12 teachers interviewed by us accepted thc sentence whereas the other six totally rejected it.

Interestingly, 12 senior teachers of Urdu (none of them has less than 12 years of teaching experience) were interviewed and a kind of opinion poll was arranged. The questionnaire was placed also before a couple of Urdu creative writers and their opinions were recorded. The methodology generally adopted was that a certain sentence carrying the expression and borrowed from some book or newspaper was put before the informant and he was asked whether he agreed that the expression was a literal translation from English. Thereafter, he was asked whether he found the expression well-formed and that whether he would accept the use of the expression in (i) informal speech, (ii) formal speech, (iii) informal writing and (iv) formal writing :

(1) aisa koi motabaadil markit meN aaya hi nahiN — No such alternative has appeared in the market — *Ajkal*, Delhi, February 1983, p. 5.

Though the use of the English word 'market' attracts attention here because it is a case of code-mixing what we find particularly significant is the use of the word 'motabaadil' which appears to be an attempt to literally translate the English word 'alternative'. Of the 12 teachers nine were of the view that the use has its source in English. A very senior teacher remarked that though the source is English the use is very prevalent in Urdu now. Another teacher said that the word though translated from English is only in scholarly use and he did not accept its use in speech, formal or informal. Another informant told us that the word was from English and that the word previously in use was 'badal' and now 'motabaadil' was in vogue as an influence of the English language. Another teacher was of the opinion that the word was present from much before. The word may have been there already but what is important for us is the use it has been put to here. A couple of teachers did not like its use in formal speech and writing. The creative writers also thought that the word was translated from English and ascribed the use to the ceaseless search for exact equivalents and more meaningful words.

(2) kaun sii aiiTem ko laal qandiil dikhayii jaye — which item should be shown red signal — *Ajkal*, August 1983, p. 44.

Once again we feel attracted towards the English word 'item' but once again we are basically interested in the expression 'laal qandiil, which, as we think, is a translation of the English expression 'red signal'. Eleven out of 12 teachers interviewed agreed with our premise though one was of the view that the expression 'laal qandiil' was present in the Urdu language even before the British came to India. The teacher who disagreed has serious doubts about the source because he thought the showing of 'qandiil' was a pretty old practice. Six of the 12 teachers accepted its use both in speech and writing whereas 6 others totally disapproved the use in any of the four areas. The creative writers thought that the idea was from English and that the use has not caught up in speech yet.

(3) *kaam* kaaji khwatiin — working women — *Ajkal,* August 1983, p. 42 :

Seven out of 12 teachers agreed that the exprssion 'kaam kaaji khwatiin' is a direct translation of the English 'working women'. Two observed that the expression was from Hindi. However, even if it is Hindi the source ultimately is apparently English. Two others thought that it may be from English while one informant found the use wrong and bogus. One who thought that the expression was a translation from English said that previously it was 'daaiyaaN' while another considered the translated use to be 'a solid die' and said that the other possible use was 'kaarguzaar khwatiin'. Six totally disapproved the use, two allowed the use in informal speech while remaining four accepted the use in all four situations. The creative writers agreed that the expression was a clear translation and accepted it though they remarked that it was not in wide currency and that the English equivalent 'working women' was itself often used in Urdu.

(4) achhe moallim ki kaamraanii, aap ittefaq kareNge, zohnoN ko roshan karna Hae — The success of good teacher, you will agree, is in enlightening the intellect :

—chaan phatak, aap ghaur kareN, ek nehayat socha samjha amal hae — investigation, you think over it, is a highly intellectual exercise.

—in jawabaat ki roshni meN, aap mujh se ittefaaq kareNge, ilm-e-tanqiid aur aml-e-tanquiid ki moassar taaliim qatan dushwaar nahiN — in the light of these responses, you will agree with me, the effective teaching of the theory and practice of criticism is not at all difficult.

— Syed Mohammad Hasnain, *Hamaarii Zabban,* June 8, 1982 :

Eleven out of 12 teachers agreed with our standpoint that the syntax pattern here is that often used in English and they found it acceptable also. One of them said that the pattern was more or less Urdu now whereas another informant opined that though it was not urdu yest this kind of complicated structure was acceptable now. A teacher who had his doubts stressed that such structures were prevalent in old Urdu as well though he did not cite any examples. Apparently, this kind of interruption in the middle of a sentence is characteristic of English, particularly of conversational English. The creative writers also agreed that the pattern was English and approved of it.

(5) diiwaar-ta-diiwar qaaliin — wall to wall carpet — *Shama*, New Delhi, May 1983, p. 41 :

Elevan people agreed with our assumption that the expression was a translation of the much used English expression 'wall to wall carpet'. One of these teacher, however, stressed that the expression did not appear attractive enough. The teacher who disagreed said that it was not a translation but only a 'coincidence' and he said that the practice of constructing expressions with 'ta' was a vogue in Persian. He did not elaborate on his use of the term 'coincidence'. He observed that the use was not acceptable in informal speech. All other teachers found it acceptable in all situations. The creative writers also agreed that the use was a translated borrowing from English and found it acceptable.

(6) motawaazi Akaali Dal qaaim — parallel Akali Dal established — *Qaumi Awaz*, Patna, 15.5.83 :

Once again 11 out of 12 teachers said yes to our hunch that 'motawaazi' here was a simple translation of the English word 'parallel'. The twelfth teacher only said that the use appeared to him to be a translation of 'parallel', though 'motawaazi' was a very old expression. The other 11 informants accepted it in all positions. The creative writers said that it was a transalation from English and considered it acceptable in all areas.

(7) eik Himalayaii ghalti kar baithi huN — I have committed a colossal blunder — *Shama*, May 1983, p. 21 :

Our assumption was that 'Himalayaii ghalti' was a clear translation of the well-known expression in Indian English, 'Himalyan blunder' (in fact, a coinage of Gandhi) and all 12 informants agreed. Certainly 'Himalayaii ghalti' is not in large scale use. Expressions of this nature are not often heard in informal speech. 'Faash ghalti' or 'BaRii bhuul' are in general use. Interestingly, however, nine informants accepted it in informal speech and eight in all areas. The opinion of the creative writers was that the expression was from English and they found it acceptable in all situations.

(8) 'nishana' used as a synonym of the English word 'target' — nishana moqarrar kiyaa gayaa hae — *Meaar-e-qaum*, 31.1.1983 :

Nine teachers found our hunch that it was the translation of its English equivalent 'target' correct. One said it was Arabic, one that it was non-English (he did not elaborate) and one that it was actually a translation of 'hadaf' and not of English 'target'. We can perhaps easily rule our Arabic as a source here because there is hardly any Arabic around and people are hardly exposed to it. Certainly 'nishana' has been used in a sense very close to that of 'target', *e.g.*, the popular film song — kahiiN pe nigaaheN KahiiN pe nishaana. Eleven teachers considered 'nishaana' acceptable in all four positions whereas one rejected it totally. The creative writers also found it acceptable and agreed that it had its source in English.

(9) karpuurii dal Janata Party meN tahliil ho gayii — Karpoori group has been dissolved into the Janata Party — *Sangam*, Patna, 21.1.1983 :

(Though 'merged' appears to be a better expression, 'dissolved' is also sometimes seen). The hunch was that 'tahliil' was used as a translation of the equivalent 'dissolve'. Ten of the 12 teachers said yes but two of these 10 added that 'zam' was a better equivalent than 'tahliil' as (as one of them said) 'tahliil' involves the total loss of the thing dissolved. One of them said that 'tahliil' was not a translation of 'dissolve' whereas the other noted that the use 'tahliil' was not anything new and that it has come to Urdu via Persian and Arabic. Seven out of 12 accepted its use in all situations, four rejected its use outright while one of them allowed its use in speech only, formal and informal. The creative writers agreed that the use came from English through translation and accepted it. It was argued by one that the sentence itself was wrong because 'dal' was masculine and not feminine.

(10) jamhuuriyat ke taaboot meN aakhri kiil thoNk diya — the last nail was hit into the coffin of democracy — *Sangam*, Patna, 10.8.1982 :

The obvious premise was that the construction 'taaboot meN aakhri kiil thoNkna' was a literal translation of a very common English use 'hitting the last nail into the coffin'. As expected, all 12 people interviewed agreed, 11 accepted its use in all four areas whereas one accepted it only in writing, formal and informal. The creative writers agreed with our assumption and accepted its use. One of our informants found the sentence wrong, as he said, 'kiil' was not masculine.

(11) shimlaa jazbaa — Simla spirit — *Qaumi Awaz*, Patna, 7.2.1982 :

The hunch was that 'shimlaa jazbaa' was a translation of the much used 'Simla spirit', a favourite expression of English journalists. As expected, once again, all 12 agreed with our assumption though three said the expression was not a standard one. Four were prepared to accept it totally, six rejected its use altogether, one allowed it only in informal speech and writing whereas one was willing to accept it in writing alone.

According to one of them, a better equivalent of 'spirit' may be 'fikr' or 'khayaal' in Urdu. The creative writers thought it came from English and found it acceptable.

(12) jamhuuri nizaam qaaem kar ke samaaji *naabaraabarii* aur istehsal ko maut ke ghaat utaarne ki tadbiireN amal meN layii gayiiN — after establishing a democractic system ways and means were adopted to bring an end to inequality and exploitation — Syed Mohammad Mohsin, *Ajkal*, August 1982, p. 41 :

The issue here is the use of 'naabaraabarii' for which there is already an expression in use in Urdu, *i.e.*, 'adam mosawaat. The premise was that 'naabaraabarii' was used as an influence of the English word 'inequality' and 10 out of 12 agreed though one of them added that it may be an influence of Hindi. Hindi, however, does not use 'naabaraabarii' for inequality. One of these teachers remarked that it had not come from English and that is was Urdu. Another teacher said that it was Urdu and in use because of the tendency to simplify Urdu. Ten of them were willing to accept its use in all four positions whereas one was prepared to accept its use only in informal speech and the other only in formal speech and writing. The creative writers too agreed with our hunch and favoured its use. They, however, found it strange that a simple word, *naabaraabarii* was used for 'adam mosawaat' in the sentence cited here whereas 'istehsaal' was retained.

(13) notis bahut mokhtasar mila hae — we have been given a short notice — *Maulaana* by Shaukat Thaanvii :

Certainly this sentence has been written bearing in mind the English phrase 'short notice' and our informants agreed that it was so but six of them emphasized that the translation was not accurate, that it lacked clarity here, that it was not in keeping with the temperament of the Urdu language. The use is definitely vague though it has come from a very important writer. Eight teachers found it totally unacceptable, four accepted it in formal speech. The creative writers also did not consider it a good translation and found it unacceptable.

(14) agar maeN ghalat nahiN huuN to — if I am not wrong — Khaliq Anjum — *Hamaari Zabaan*, New Delhi, 22.3.1984 :

We started with the assumption that the expression was used with the famous English use 'if I am not wrong' always at the back of writer's mind. Eleven out of 12 informants were also of the same view while the twelfth said that it was not English and that it was in keeping with the Urdu grammar. To nine of them the use was acceptable in all 4 positions.

One found it absolutely unacceptable whereas two others showed their readiness to accept it in informal speech and writing alone. The creative writers did not find it likeable enough and were not ready to accept it anywhere.

(15) ba moqaabal — *vs.* — Q*aumi Awaz*, Patna, 8.4.1985 :

The hypothesis here was 'ba moqaabla' always brought the English 'vs.' to mind and was perhaps a translation of the English expression. Nine out of 12 teachers accepted this proposition, two thought that it was Persian and one that it was non-English. The word was acceptable to all of them and in all situations. The same was the view of the creative writers as well — that it was English but acceptable.

(16) urdwaane ka amal jaari kiya — the process of Urduization was started — Gian Chand, *Lesaani Motaale*, p. 195 :

The hunch was the 'urdwana' was actually a translation of 'Urduization', an expression coined on the pattern of 'anglicization'. Ten thought it was so — one went to the extent of informing us that actually it was Brajmohan Datatarya 'Kaifi' who started using this kind of verb in Urdu. One thought it was English though not a good construction, one that it was Arabic and one that such a use was prevalent in Persian. Three did not accept it all all, six accepted it in all positions, one only in informal speech and writing, one only in writing and one only in speech. The creative writers thought it was English — that previously 'jaama pahara diyaa gayaa', was in use in Urdu but that was rather wordy. They accepted 'urdwana' in all kinds of speech and writing.

(17) na jang moaahde — no-war pact — *Sangam*, Patna, 10.7.1982 :

Undoubtedly, 'na-jang moaahde' is apparently a direct borrowing in a translated form from the English equivalent 'no-war pact' and, as expected, all 12 teachers agreed with our stand. In much the same way, we find these days the use 'naamaajriyat' for plotless. The use of 'na jang moaahde' is acceptable to all the teachers and in all situations. The same was the reaction of the creative writers also.

(18) aaj shaam eik jalsa hone ja raha hae — a meeting is going to be held this evening — an announcement :

This kind of construction is very common these days and we suppose that 'hone ja raha hae' is translated form of English 'going to be held'. Ten out of 12 agreed that it was a translation, two said that it was not so whereas one said that it was heard only in colloquial speech though he, too, agreed that it was occasionally seen in writing also. Nine will accept it in all four situations, two only in speech, informal and formal and one only in informal speech. The creative writers found themselves in agreement with our hypothesis and accepted the use in all four areas. A noted writer of fiction in Urdu, Ghyas Ahmed Gaddi has used the expression (in one of his short stories) — 'batane jaa rahi thi' instead of 'bataane waalii thii'.

(19) voh apne kharch se London shahar *ko* gaya — he went to the city of London at his own expense :

hazaaroN miil ka safar kar ke voh Delhi *ko* laut aaye haeN — he has returned to Delhi after covering thousands of miles :

Our point here was that *ko* in *London shahar ko* and *Delhi ko* is there because of the influence of English where 'to' is used in these circumstances — *i.e.*, 'to the city of London', 'to Delhi', etc. Ten found it there as an influence of English — of these nine considered it to be wrong and not standard, one said that such a use was not Urdu, two said that the sentence was all right without 'ko' and that 'ko' was redundant. One informant stressed that linguists and people who are supposed to know generally do not use it at the literary level. The remaining two found it 'regional' and remarked that it was in use because of the local impact. Four of them showed there willingness to accept this kind of use in any position, six rejected it outright, one said he would accept it only in informal speech and writing and one in all areas except in formal writing. The creative writers did not accept it in any situation though they observed that 'ko' was being increasingly used these days in certain areas.

(20) sunte haeN *ke* — kahte haeN *ke*, suna jaata hae *ke* — kaha jaata hae *ke* :

It is heard that, it is said that ... :

Our standpoint was that the use of 'ke' in these sentences was in practice under the influence of English 'that'. These sentences are not rendered deficient in any way even if we drop 'ke'. Six informants agreed that 'ke' was there as an influence of English, two said that English had nothing to do with '*ke*' here. Two emphatically said that 'ke' was very much Urdu and was often found in pretty old writings and consequently they found it difficult to agree with our premise. Once of them was of the view that it was only a kind of resemblance and stressed that 'ke' was present even in the writings of Meer Amman (late eighteenth century) but even he could not help adding that there was definitely some impact of English some time because the pattern was that of English. To all 12 the use was acceptable. The creative writers did not subscribe to this view —

that 'ke' was in use because of the influence of the English language. They, too, however, would accept it in all areas.

(21) jahaaN unke waalid ne eik zamiin khariid lii — where his father bought a land — eik kitaab naagri rasmulkhat me hae — a book is in Nagri script :

The point brought to the fore here by us was that *eik zamiin* and *eik kitaab* are not actually Urdu and that the use of 'eik' here was under the direct influence of English where 'a' in such cases in a syntactic requirement. Eight teachers agreed that 'eik' was used here due to English, two had their doubts, one said that it was Arabic and one emphasized that the concept of 'eik' in such constructions was already present in Urdu and was not anything new. It was emphasized that those who speak standard language do not use it and that it was not in general use. Nine accepted it in all areas, two rejected it straight while one allowed it only in speech. By and large, 'eik' was considered something additional and useless. The creative writers also found it serving no purpose and something that was not going to last. They found it totally unacceptable.

(22) subject yaani mauzuu — Wahab Ashrafi in *Maani Ki Talash* : misunderstanding yaani ghalat fahmi — Shaukat Thaanvi in *Maulaana* :

What we see in the above two expressions is that though used by Urdu writers they carry English equivalents first and the writers have gone on thereafter to give their Urdu equivalents. The present writer has called the uses of this kind 'emphatic communion' (1983 : 114) — they are used for elaboration, clarification and emphasis. Eight people said they would accept the use of this type, two only in formal speech and writing, one only in speech and one was prepared to accept it only in informal speech. Though the creative writers were not unwilling to accept it they did not like it.

(23) fursat hi fursat ho, time hi time ho — when there is a lot of leisure — Fikr Taunsvi, *Aawaz,* New Delhi, 16.7.1983; apna martabba — apna status — *Ajkal,* August 1983, p. 43; achhi baat kahi — well said — Shaukat Thaanvi in *Maulaana* :

These once again may be considered to be instances of 'emphatic communion' though the word order has been reversed. The Urdu expression precedes the English one here. Nine teachers accepted it, one rejected it thoroughly, one was willing to accept it only in speech and one only in informal writing. During the interview, a teacher pronounced the expression as something 'nonsensical', as something that betrayed a lack of confidence in the language in which the writing was being done. Another found it clumsy and pointed out that not many people actually used it in practice. His suggestion was that the English equivalents should be placed within brackets. The present writer, however, finds the use of this nature very common in Urdu speech and writing. It was also remarked that such uses were confined to course books (which apparently is not wholly true). However, it was rightly stated by one of our informants that a use like this was elucidatory. The creative writers also did not favour these uses and noted in particular that they hardly served any purpose. They did not find them acceptable either.

The results of the study show that the Urdu language is very receptive and open to change and, like any other language, is consistently growing and changing and adapting itself to new environments. A look at the social change, it must be stressed, is necessary in order to account for the changes. The study shows that teachers as well as the creative writers in Urdu, the latter more than the former, have of late been very liberal. Though generally conceding that these expressions have been translated from English most of them found them acceptable. This clearly reveals their eagerness to enrich their language. That they often look towards English for this purpose is evident from this study. Not that all of these expressions were not there in Urdu before but the way they have been used in the instances cited in the foregoing discussions was important. Some of them may not be new in form but are perhaps new in function. They are sometimes neologisms and catch our attention. The Urdu language has incorporated a number of proverbs, etc., concerned with the changing perspective. Such uses are often seen in journalistic writings which, as many assert, may not perhaps be considered to be standard — some of them appear in newspaper headlines, *e.g.*, 'shimlaa jazbaa' for 'Simla spirit'. However, it may be added here that in the present study we have quoted a number of examples from creative writings as well.

REFERENCES

Alam, Qaiser Zoha. *Issues* : *Linguistic and Pedagogic*, New Delhi : Sterling, 1983.

Chand, Gyan. "*Kuch Jaali KitaboN Ke Baare MeN,*" *Hamaari Zabaan*, New Delhi, October 22, 1986.

Sinha, A.K. On some Influence of English on Hindi Syntax. Paper presented at the Second International Conference on South Asian Languages and Linguistics : Hyderabad, January 9-11, 1980.

Chapter 8

ENGLISH IDIOMS AND PHRASES IN MODERN URDU LITERATURE

In 'An Aspect of the Impact of English on Urdu' I have studied the words and expressions about which my hunch is that they have been translated from English into Urdu and are being used by Urdu writers and journalists *e.g.*, mae eik mushkil laRkee hooN (Intezar Husain, 1984, p. 119). A number of expressions of this kind are now in use on a large scale in Urdu. The present study may be considered as an extension of the 1988 one although the main emphasis here is on idioms, phrases and proverbs. My earlier studies (1983, 1988) have shown that Urdu language is receptive and eager to enrich itself and that it often looks towards English for this purpose. We find here, once again, that Urdu writers and journalists often use the translated versions of English idioms and phrases.

Mrs. Manik Dhondy, in Quratulain Haider's novel *Chandni Begum* (1990), has modified her language as per the needs of her Urdu speaking in-laws and speaks Urdu fluently by literally translating English phrases and idioms. Consequently, the language that she produces is unusual and, in many ways, startling and Quratulain herself calls it 'laajawab'. When the maid servant brings the tea tray and places the same on the table, Manikbai addresses Safia thus : 'Faini bitiya — tum izzat karo'. Safia Sultana was baffled though she was used to Mrs. Dhondy's brand of Urdu. But soon she realized, 'Oho, yeh doing the honours kaa lafzee tarjuma tha'. Mrs. Dhony further said, 'mae umeed kartee HooN donkey bachhe ke tum Pakistan me bahut accha karte hoge' *i.e.* doing well. Mrs. Dhondy goes on to say —'bechaare Bobby kee pahlee shaadee chattanoN per gayee — doosree bhi bahut kuch aarzoo ke liye chhoRtee hae but tumhaare uncle Vicky kee second marriage bahut acchee jaa rahee hae'. Another original and interesting statement made by Mrs. Dhondy is : 'jaa kar pahle apna munh karo. tum zameen me kisi cheez kee tarah nahee lag rahee ho'. The person addressed, Mahnaz, got the point — 'Do your face first. You are looking like nothing on earth'. At one place in the novel, Mrs. Dhondy remarks — 'ab tum koyee bahaar ke mausam kee murghee ka bacchha nahee' — the literal translation or explanation of 'spring chicken'. In the novel she always referred to Ten Katori House as the Cup House. This use in the same novel also catches attention — 'voh eik kaala ghoDa hae' (*i.e.* Dark Horse). Abdul Moghni (1991), while reviewing *Chandni Begum*, mentions 'talking with tongue-in-cheek' but, significantly, thinks it necessary to mention the English phrase within brackets. Fowler has mentioned this phrase as a cliche.

Needless to add, all these are very interesting and meaningful instances but, as a matter of fact, have been used consciously and often their English equivalents too have been mentioned. In this note, however, I plan to take up, in particular, those expressions of this nature which are used, largely speaking, unconsciously and spontaneously and which let us know how new idioms and phrases enter a language and how educated users of the receiving language accept and take to them. It is also true, at the same time, however, that some of these expressions may not be easily intelligible to some speakers of the language specially those whose grip over both languages is not equally strong and effective. It should also be noted here that some of these expressions have hardened into just cliches in English because of overuse. The expressions which catch on and are used widely get into and become part of the receiving language.

When the poet says :

> nazar aata hae mujhe is me tamasha-e-jahaN
> is ko ei tang nazar chaae kee payalee na samajh
>
> (I find in it the spectacle of the whole universe
> You are narrow-minded if you take it only as a tea-cup)

the reader or the listener is at once reminded of the famous English expression regarding the tea-cup which presumsbly must have been at the back of the poet's mind.

'kishtiyaN jala dena' is another expression which deserves a detailed treatment here. This expression perhaps travelled from the east to the west but these days it is being very widely used in Urdu once again. It appears a correct assessment, to a large extent, that the recent appearance of this use in Urdu has been through English. It was around 8th century A.D. that Tariq and Abdurrahman had burnt their boats to ashes after entering Spain.

In Urdu Iqbal and Shibli have also used this idiom. Manohar Malgonkar writes in his novel *Spy in Amber* (p. 126) : 'You burnt your boats the moment you began behaving like a cheap little whore'. In

English 'burning the birdges' is also sometimes used and carries, more or less, the same sense. In Santha Rama Rai's *The Adventuress* (1973, p. 287) we find that when Kay says, 'I really don't know what to do next' Maria asks her 'Burnt your bridges?' Although 'burning boats' is not really an absolutely new expression by any standard for Urdu the fact remains that of late it is being used very often :

> chand saal baad waapas aae to Pakistan se bahut khafa the magar yehaN apni kishtiyaN jala chuke the is liye phir unheN waapas jaana paDa (*Khwab Baaqi HaiN*, Aley Ahmad Soroor, p. 146).

What Soroor means to suggest is that all the means and avenues were blocked for the person. Quratulain has used this expression again and again :

> tab Waahid use baDe pyar se samjhaata — tum apni kishtiyaN jala chuki ho. ab Qaasim se laDai jhagDe shroo na kar dena (*Chaae ke Baagh*, p. 43)

> use Waahid ki baat yaad ayee ke voh apni kishtiyaN jala chuki hae (*Chaae ke Baagh*, p. 56)

> tum to jaisa tum ne bataaya Jaipur me apni kishtiyaN jala ayeeN (*Gardish-e-Rang-Chaman*, p. 242)

Abdus Samad too has used this expression several times in his novel *Do Gaz Zameen*

> UnhoN ne Asghar Husain ko rokne ki har mumkin koshish kee, lekin voh to apni kishtiyaN jala chuke the. Jaane ke siwa unke paas koee chaara na tha (p. 45).

> bahut se log to zyaada paisoN ke wade par aaye lekin tawaqqa se kam paise unheN mil rahe haeN. lekin voh apni kishtiyan jala chuke haeN (p. 285).

This idiom often needs a little explanation to average readers as it may create some difficulty for them. The same can be said about the following use also :

> nayee peeDHee kee chhokri phaoRe ko phaoRa pukaarne waalee (*Chandni Begam*, Quratulain Haider, p. 375).

Aley Ahmad Soroor writes in *Khwab Baaqi HaiN* :

> bere ne poochha ke French coffee pasand karenge yaa turkee coffee. mae ne socha roma me ho to roma kee see karo, chunanche Turkish coffee ka order de diya (p. 252)

Soroor's use is an instance of direct translation of an idiom in use in

English although in Urdu there is a pointed equivalent available *i.e.* jaisa deis waisa bheis.

This construction used by Ismat Chughtaai in *Junglee Kabootar* — abhee loha garam garam hae (p. 52) and by Abdus Samad in *khwaboN ka Savera* (1994) — Afaaq ne Loha garam dekh kar ek zarb laga dee (p. 163) — is also a relevant example. When Abdus Samad writes this in *Do Gaz Zameen* — 'Mohammad Yunus khat paakar khush to bahut hue ke chalo baraf to pighlee' (p. 63) obviously he must have been thinking in terms of the equivalent English idiom. Nizam Siddiqui has written at a place in his article 'Nae Ahad kee Takhleeqeeyat' (1992) — 'nit naye mauzooaat kee kuNwaaree baraf toR rahee hae'. Although there is no doubt that the phrase 'kuNwaaree baraf' is a translation from English it looks contrived and tacked on.

The following use of Abdus Samad is now widely understood and should also be cited here :

> dar asl Hamid ko yeh ta'ajjub tha ke Akhtar Husain ne itni aasaanee ke saath use sabz jhundee kaise dikha dee thee (*Do Gaz Zameen*, p. 166).

I have quoted (1988) from the Urdu monthly *Aajkal* : 'kaun see aitem ko laal qandeel dikhayee jaye'. Seen in this perspective the use of 'sabz jhundee' catches special attention and acquires significance. This excerpt from Abdus Samad's *Do Gaz Zameen* is also an instance of external borrowing :

> bahaar ki feza aur rung me rattee baraabar bhee farq nahee aaya tha. hawa waise hi bah rahee thee aur nadiyoN me hasb maamool bahut saara paani bah chuka tha (p. 240).

It should be pointed out here, however, that this use has not yet become as common as 'sabz jhundee' and, consequently, must be causing some confusion and difficulty in respect of communication. The following, once again, from Abdus Samad, is in almost the same vein :

> afsos is ka hua ke us tanzeem ko khaak chaatnee paRee jo kabhee Hindustani awaam ke dil kee dhaRkan thee (*Do Gaz Zameen*, p. 271).

Quratulain Haider has translated almost verbatim an English expression in the following dialogue :

> begam sahiba aaj Zafarpoor tashreef le ja rahee haeN kisi ghareeb laRkee ke talaash me
> yehaaN kuchh kamee hae

> farmatee haen charity ghar se shroo honee chaahiye *(Chandni Begam*, p. 17).

The same idiom has been used by Razia Fasih Ahmad (1989) :

> angrezee kee misl hae tayee amma ke khairat apne ghar se shroo hotee hae

In his novel, *Bolo Mat Chup Raho* (1990), Husainul Haque has invented the construction 'be reeRh kee qaum' but it does not appear to be a reasonably accurate and convincing equivalent of the English expression 'spineless'.

Musharraf Alam Zauqi too has translated an English idiom but the idiom is in very common use in Urdu now and is easily understood :

> kuchh der ke liye baRee bee ka sar chakra gaya. billi ke gale me ghantee kaun baandhe.

This use of Mushtaq Ahmad Yusufi (1990) is also relevant here :

> Mirza Abdul Wadood Beg ko ghubaare puncture karne kee baRee buree aadat hae *(Aab-e-Gum*, p. 99).

These writers are actually bilinguals and are often engaged in English studies as well. In English syllabuses in our schools and colleges phrases, idioms and proverbs are given special attention. That is why, when they speak and write in Urdu they come back to their mind, again and again and, as a result, sometimes the translated equivalents of the idioms and phrases are used. At the same time, perhaps this facilitates the task of the writers — they are able to say things with greater economy, ease, point and sharpness. It is true, however, that at the time of reading (or listening) the bilingual readers (or listeners) are often reminded of the original English uses.

REFERENCES

Alam, Qaiser Zoha, 1983. *Issues : Linguistic and Pedagogic*. New Delhi : Sterling.

——, 1988. An Aspect of the Impact of English on Urdu. *Indian Linguistics*, Pune. March-December. Vol. 49.

Chughtai, Ismat. *Junglee Kabootar*. Delhi : Hind Pocket Books.

Fasih Ahmad, Razia, 1989. Phulwari. *BiswiN Sadi*. Delhi : Hind-o-Pak Adab Number.

Haider, Quratulain, 1965. *Chae ke Bagh*. Bombay : Halqa-e-Adab.

——, 1988. *Gardish-e-Rang-e-Chaman*. Delhi : Educational Publishing House.

——, 1990. *Chandni Begam*. Delhi : Educational Publishing House.

Haque, Husainul, 1990. *Bolo Mat Chup Raho.* Lucknow : Nusrat Publishers.

Husain, Intezar, 1984 edition. *Bustee*. Lahore : Sang-e-Meel Publications.

Malgonkar, Manohar. *Spy in Amber.* Delhi : Orient Paperbacks.

Moghni, Abdul, 1991. 'Chandni Begam : A Review'. *Aiwan-e-Urdu*. August. New Delhi.

Rama Rau, Santha, 1973. *The Adventuress.* Delhi : Hind Pocket Books.

Samad, Abdus, 1988. *Do Gaz Zameen.* Delhi : SK Offset Printers.

——, 1994. *KhwaboN ka Savera*, Patna.

Siddiqui, Nizam, 1992, *Naye Ahad Ki Takhleeqeeyat.* Tawazun. Malegaon, 23-24.

Soroor, Aley Ahmad, 1991. *Khwab Baqee HaiN.* Aligarh : Educational Book House.

Yusufi, Mushtaq Ahmad, 1990. *Aab-e-Gum.* Hyderabad : Hesami Book Depot.

Zauqi, Mosharraf Alam. 'Zanankhana'. *Zoboan-o-Adab*. Patna, Vol. 18. 1 & 2.

"Mr. Arif, do you play?"

"Yes, Farkhunda Apa."

"What?"

"Cricket."

"Oh — I mean any instruments like violin or piano — I love piano."

"Mr. Arif."

(CheeNkeN) — "er — Farkhunda Apa — mujhe baRa sakht zukam ho raha hae — kahiN aap ko na lag jaaye" (sneezes — "er — Farkhunda Apa — I am suffering from a severe cold. Maybe you'll catch it".)

"Oh, no ...".

The following are some other examples of sentential switches:

— "It's a gala day today ... aao baitho aaj donoN mil kar ise celebrate kareNge" ("Come and sit, we will celebrate it together") – KKK.

— "A woman's psychology always depends upon her biology" – MZ

— "It's a boy"

"Congratulations" — BYB

— "You think you are very smart" — LKSR

— "What a joke my aunty" — SKD

— "Can you tell me why I am so smart?" — SKD

— "Why are you sleeping, donkey?" — SKD

— "Can I help you, darling?"

"No, Mrs. Josephine, thank you ..." — PC

The Urdu writers have often described in English what has been called "Phatic communion". For commands, requests and address forms etc. English is used over and over again — the switch here gives expression to emotional overtones. In fact, codes are frequently mixed to express emotions and feelings — by God (BSS), thanks ever so much, cheerio (MBSK), shut up, my sweety, my darling, thank you (PC), well sir (MPM), God is great (S), yes sir, O.K., hi, bi and 'how are you'. Sometimes the mixing of this kind indicates 'distance' and 'formality' (Sridhar : 1978), 'strangeness' and 'alienation' (Keller), 'emphasis' (Southworth : 1977).

We often come across the lexical and phrasal switches also. Most of the lexical switches are connected with the noun, verb and adjective. The lexical items are freely borrowed from English (into Urdu). Interesting phrases are formed joining items of both languages. Many a time the following device is used : Urdu/English modifier+Urdu/English headword+Urdu/English qualifier. These writers evidently attempt to modify Urdu nouns with English adjectives and English nouns with Urdu adjectives. This kind of formal syntactic quality often becomes an important artistic point. Many of the following examples fit into this scheme fully or partially. It may be noted that a special feature of these examples is hybridization (Urdu+English) : shaandaar pageant, seyaah hood (JTGC), himaaqat zada cookery book, nafees sa lecture, nafees impression, marmareeN porch, neele rang ka tunic, neelgoN swimming pool, rangeen shade (SR), mustaid reporter, kaam ka overcoat, brown rang ki sheep skin jacket, society ke taaza tareen scandals, shaadi karne waala type, khaandaani politics (ABHSIK), badrang furniture, ghair maamuli gazaette (MNLKBS), insaani anatomy, nafsayaati complex, behad charming (CKB), Bengali jeweller (DJ), nayee scheme, booRha refugee (MPM), naakaara negative (IKQ), etc.

Not infrequently, English modifiers are attached to Urdu headwords (English+Urdu) : French cut darhi (EDC), German moseeqi (JTGC), pantry ke darwaaze, immature dimagh, adventures ki kahaaniyaN, metaphysical patangeN, chocolate ke guRiyaghar, tragic shakhsiyateN (SR), indoor qism ke mashghale, courtyards ke pokhta farsh, diplomatic guftagu, shares ki qimateN, typical qism ka shauhar, artistic mizaaj (ABHSIK), original kaam, streamlined badmaashi, highbrow naqqaad (MNLKBS), scottish joRa (CKB) and toilet mez (BSS) are some relevant examples.

The adjective phrases 'very sorry' and 'very rare' (English+English) etc. are prevalent in Urdu and occasionally 'bahut rare' (Urdu+English) also but phrases like 'very dukhi' are never heard. The English adverbs are also used with Urdu words *e.g.*, 'kaafi early' and 'bahut late' (Urdu+English) etc. In much the same way, 'generally' and 'completely' are also widely used. The speakers of Urdu easily and frankly construct verb formations with the help of English words. For example; programme banana (YKEDJ), strike kareNge (JW), retire ho gaye (LL) and reserve karaana (JTGC) — v+operator. But English words are not frequently used with English helping verbs in Urdu conversations. Such English words as 'enjoy' (HS), 'test' (MNLKBS), 'start', 'drive' (CKB), 'fascinate', 'co-opt' (KJDH) and 'receive' (UUS) are often used as verbs in Urdu.

A very common way of forming words in this mixed language is that morphemic changes are made by attaching Urdu suffixes to English words — they undergo the inflectional processes of Urdu. For instance, boreyat

(SR), recordoN (S), partiyaN (ABHSIK), cardoN (MNLKBS), appealoN (S), schemeN (H), refugeeoN (EDC), tubeN (UUS), degreeyaN (JKPAC), afsaroN (PC), cluboN, seatoN (KJDH), busoN, motroN, tyroN (RKP) etc. Mention may be made here of 'fuse shuda' ('fused') used by RL in IKQ. Quite often, English words are also used with English suffixes (English+English) *e.g.*, Spanish waltz (JTGC), adventures, American (SR), shares, scandals, artistic, morals, studios, courtyards (ABHSIK), good lookers, ringleaders, pictures, classical quotations, semi-finals, singles, lectures, lineswoman, wardens, streamlined (MNLKBS), plantations (CKB), agitators, holiday makers, undergraduates, lords, ladies, stored, cells, movies (LL), models, decorators, ideals (DBDYBY), attached, customs, confused, searchlights, Irish, values (KJDH), boy friends (PC), nickel-plated (IKQ), higher studies (H), state gardens, arms dealer (AD), retired (GP), depressed (HS) etc. Sometimes one finds English suffixes added to Urdu names and words e.g., Arjumand's crowd (ABHSIK). Thus we see that English suffixes are attached to Urdu words and Urdu suffixes to English words to obtain plural forms. In particular, English plural forms often appear in Urdu. The English affixes, many a time, are retained in the negative expressions as well *e.g.*, unfit (GP), unsporting (MNLKBS) etc.

Another interesting feature of the mixed language is that often both parts of the phrase are English (English+English) *e.g.*, Virgin Mary, Sweet Jesus, sports car (JTGC), bird watching (DW), heart fail (SR), off duty, Radio fan (ABHSIK), ladylike, wire pulling, classical quotations, moral support (MNLKBS and DFKD), scandal mongering (DBDYBY), old maid (HS), tea research, telephone system (CKB), peacock green (IKQ), modern lover (RKP), literary craze, future shock, culture transfer, decadent Western European, hit star, night life, honorary cousin, left wing, human decency (KJDH) etc. It should be stressed here that very often the different elements of these phrases go together and are complementary to each other. Let us cite some examples : sky scraper, bay window, common room, swimming pool, at home, visitors' room, civil list, writing pad, dining hall, black mailing, sportsman, week-end, stand bye, super intellectual, palm grove, dressing gown, foreign service (MNLKBS), garden party, drama programme, bank clerk, news stand, grand concert (LL), flash back (CKB), bed room, stock exchange (ABHSIK), bank balance, extra girl, outdoor shooting, electric fan, cinema building, cinema gate, booking office, black market (MPH), night show, first show, grandfather (BSS), boy friend, girl friend, fry pan (PC), lamp post (SKD), Victoria Cross, group photo, flash bulb, business magazine, traffic constable (IKQ), civil defence, table lamp (AMKHS), smoking pipe, central government, house allowance (H), city bus (RKP), chief clerk, police ground, postal inspector (EDC), beauty queen (UUS), power house (KK) and double century (AD). The English phrases connected with sports and games are used in Urdu without any hesitation. For example, only in AD, RL has mentioned 'team', 'partnership', 'stump out', 'wicket', 'score', 'duck', 'bowling' etc. The same can be said about the designations of the posts.

Now and then, Urdu prepositions join English words (English+Urdu prep+English) *e.g.*, showman ka carnival (SR), college ki term (MNLKBS), flash back dar flash back, lunch ka order (CKB), nickelplated tasweer waale frame, cathedral ka ball, photography ka art (IKQ), bus stand ki railing, central jail ka bus stop (RKP), wireless ka mechanic (GP), gray colour ka half coat (UUS) etc. In fact, words and phrases are borrowed from English freely and used in Urdu conversation (direct transfers) *e.g.*, dormitory, floor (JTGC), fraud (KJDH), nursery, propose, professional (SR), tragedy (ABHSIK), study, cousin, salute, profile, referee, wedding, shooting, announce, script, shock, vision (MNLKBS), ultimatum, parasite (CKB), picketing (JW), confusion, publicity, cabinet, nostalgia, skit, aristocracy, progressive, countryside, practical, colonial, landlady (LL), portrait, literature, politics, background, appreciate, cynic, glamorous, goodwill (DBDYBY), stand, chauffeur (MPM), waltz, jealous (JKPAC), moonlight and shadow (DJ), backyard, contrast, condemn, wave (IKQ), headquarters, fly (AMKHS), guide, deputy, competition, transport (H), workshop (GP), hairdo, strange (UUS), accident, toast, fountain pen (AO), postman, airgun (KK), track, footboard (T) and draft (S) etc. Importantly, the equivalents of many of these words and phrases are available in Urdu but even then they find their way into conversations among the bilinguals.

Code-switching is, in fact, an important and unavoidable element of the speech of the bilinguals. When these writers depict the urban life they use the very language which the educated urban people actually speak. The switches in these writings, therefore, present the real situation. Order (in place of 'tarteeb') (GTGC), super qism ki (SR), indoor qism ke mashghale, how fantastic, season had se zyada dull, Arjun Garh state ki policy, recordoN ka announcement (ABHSIK), drama stage karne ki shauqeen (SR), central aur provincial devta, how sweet, how dashing, unsporting my foot (MNLKBS), Ph. D. my foot (DBDYBY), beghair press kiye kapre (S) etc. are some phrases which the bilinguals often use in their everyday speech. At times, they create 'bilingual portmanteau words'. For example, an English word is used with Urdu shortening — 'intellectui' from 'intellectual' (DBDYBY). Frequently, English words are used by way of elucidation, over and above the Urdu word — "Yeh waqea ke Rahat ne mujhe ghusul khaane me bulaaya us ki jismaani *numaish pasandi yaani exhibitionism* ka ghammaz tha" (The fact that Rahat called me into her bathroom bears testimony to her physical exhibitionism) — (CKB). To be true, the bilinguals often make such statements. In so far as the terminology is concerned, why not name it Emphatic Communion? Rightly, sometimes we feel as if no exact equivalents of the English terms were available in Urdu. Naturally, therefore, English terms are preferred in these situations — in the place of difficult and not-so-happy Urdu terms or to neutralise their effect. Apparently, the following statements from DBDYBY have been borrowed directly from the real-life-situation conversations among the bilinguals :

— Trnity College – hoNh – fiddlesticks.

— Baithe bethaye is qisse me involve ho gaya.

— Behad matter of fact andaaz me us ne baat shru ki.

— Apne saare manners saari tahzeeb saara reserve bhool kar voh bachhoN ki tarah pukaarne laga.

or the following from SR :

— Tum eik pseudo duniya me rahte ho.

or these from KJDH :

— Kya waqai ham apni bus miss kar chuke haiN?

— On the whole sabhi achhe ja rahe haeN.

— Frontiers of knowledge wasee tar hote ja rahe haeN.

— Out of date ho chuke haeN.

or this from IKQ :

— Good morning, mae Atiya Mohiuddin hooN — kya aap meri friends ka eik snap leNge? Us kone me aa jaaiye jahaN zayaafat ka saamaan chuna hua hae. Thanks (Good morning. I am Atiya Mohiuddin. Would you take a snap of my friends? Please come to the corner where dining tables have been arranged).

It should also be noted here in passing that the bilinguals freely speak the English technical terms.

It is worth mentioning that this kind of code-switching is not confined to prose alone. We get numerous examples of code-switching in Urdu poetry also. The comic poets have often made us laugh heartily by making a judicious use of English words and phrases :

Allotment ke is daur me Majeed mujhe
Makaan mil na saka shaeri allot hui — Majeed Lahauri
(In this age of allotments I could only be allotted poetry and not a house).

Of late, there has been a noticeable tendency in the serious modern Urdu poetry, too, to use English terms. Forster (1971) has referred to bilingual or multilingual verses in European literature of the Middle Ages and the Renaissance. He says, "It is a phenomenon easily occurring in conditions of bilingualism and diglossia". Forster asserts that a poet might blatantly show off his multilingual accomplishment, as in the case of Oswald von Wolkenstein using six languages in a single poem. The 'macaronic' verse is an extreme example of the blending of two languages in poetry. The current Indian scene is replete with varieties of bilingual and multilingual verses. Forster cites Eliot's *The Wasteland,* Pound's *Cantos*, and Joyce's *Ulysses* and *Finnegans Wake* as outstanding specimens of polyglot literature.

Not surprisingly, many English words and phrases have almost been transferred to Urdu. That is why, most of the Urdu writers use them with a view to bringing their writings close to reality. In the daily speech of these bilinguals English words are used not only in their root forms but also with various kinds of morphemic and syntactic transformations — with suffixes and prefixes *e.g.*, play (verb), player (noun), kindly (adverb), childish (adjective), unfit (negative), singers (plural) and retired (past) etc. Let it be mentioned here that these writers occasionally use the wrong forms of these expressions or the incorrect pronunciation of them (RL has written 'stump out' instead of 'stumped out' in AD, GAG 'gra : nd father' instead of 'grændfather').

English has been in use in our country as a second language and has gone deep into the culture of the bilinguals and is now an essential inherent part of it. The English words and phrases have entered into their total linguistic repertoire. That is why, in spite of the presence of Urdu equivalents the bilinguals use these English words to give exact expression to the overtones and undertones of their thoughts and feelings, to describe them with the appropriate emphasis and to make their statements more effective. No doubt, as many say, often the reason for this mixing is 'linguistic elitism' for in our urban culture English still retains a powerful and prestigious position. This kind of switching and mixing perhaps gives rise to a new variety of language. The educated people, the people under

Western influence and the people having status in society generally speak this kind of language. This language is widely used in offices, educational institutions, parties, picnics, meetings, discussions, greeting, thanksgiving, leave taking etc. This culture may reasonably be called a bilingual culture. Perhaps (as Keller has also remarked) here we find not only bilingualism but also, what would be more correctly called 'biculturalism and cross-cultural contrasts'. As Verma (1977) says, it tends to "generate a new unified system of code externalizing not two separate cultures but a new system of socio-cultural values". This kind of language is often used for ironic or satirical purposes and also for deliberately drawing attention to itself (as Roman Jakobson has said). Code-switching is so radical a phenomenon that, according to Keller, in itself it constitutes 'foregrounding' (with some compelling motive), Keller is not off the mark when he says that if code-switching is indeed "strong medicine", then it should be used sparingly, because code-switching carries with it the solemn duty of providing for its "esthetic adequacy". It should be realized, however, that most of the people who are shown switching codes in these writings are, in fact, "compound bilinguals" — persons whose code-switching is beyond conscious or voluntary control.

Notes : 1. The stories and novels from which the data were obtained:

Qurratulain Haider (QH) : Housing Society (HS)
Sare Raahe (SR)
Mere Bhi Sanam Khaane (MBSK)
Jab Toofan Guzar Chuka (JTGC)
AasmaN Bhi Hae Sitam Ijaad Kya (ABHSIK)
Mae Ne LaakhoN Ke Bol Sahe (MNLKBS)
Chai Ke Baagh (CKB)
London Letter (LL)
Dajla Ba Dajla Yam Ba Yam (DBDYBY)
Yaad Ki Ek Dhunak Jale (YKEDJ)
Jila Watan (JW)
Daalan Waala (DW)
Kaare JahaN Daraz Hae (KJDH)

Ram Lal (RL) : Sannata (S)
Intezaar Ke Qaidi (IKQ)
Eik Dilkash Chehra (EDC)

	Udaas Udaas September (UUS) Hamdardi (H) Roshni Ka Phan (RKP) Aakhri Daao (AD) Gharib Parwar (GP) Andhere Me Khoi Hui Saleeb (AMKHS) Khata Kaar (KK) Aag Os (AO) Tamasha (T)
Ghyas Ahmed Gaddi (GAG):	Subh Ka Daaman (SKD) Badsoorat Sayaah Saleeb (BSS) Payaasi ChiRiya (PC) Manzoar-o-pas-e-Manzar (MPH) Dorothy Johnson (DJ) Joohi ka Pauda Aur Chaand (JKPAC) Baabe (B)
Krishn Chander (KC) :	Kaaghaz ki Naao (KKN) London Ke Saat Rang (LKSR)
Kausar Chaandpuri (KCP) :	Muskuraai Zindagi (MZ)
Rajindar Singh Bedi (RSB) :	Beewi Ya Beemaari (BYB)
Kanhaiya Lal Kapoor (KLK):	Desi Firangi Ka Darbaar (DFKD)

REFERENCES

Akere, F. 1980. "Verbal Strategies in Communal Meetings : Code-switching and Status Manipulation in a Bi-dialectal Yoruba Speech Community. *Language Sciences*. Vol. 2. No. 1.

Breitborde, L.B. 1983. "Levels of analysis in sociolinguistic explanation : bilingual code switching, social relations and domain theory" Int. J. Soc. Lang. 39.

Fishman, Joshua A. 1972. *Language in Sociocultural Change*. California : Stanford University Press.

Girdhar, P.P. 1976. The Language of Literature. *IJOAL*. Vol. II, No. 1.

Guruprasad, Thakur. 1974. "Review of Leonard Forster's The Poet's Tongue." 1971. In : *IL*. Vol. 35, No. 1.

Kachru, Braj B. 1977. "Toward Structuring Code-mixing : An Indian Perspective". In : Gopal Sharma and Suresh Kumar (eds.). *Indian Bilingualism*. Agra: Kendriya Hindi Sansthan.

Keller, Gary D. The Literary Stratagems available to the Bilingual Chicano Writer. In : Edit. F. Jimenez "The Identification and Analysis of Chicano Literature." Bilingual Press Book.

Pathak, R.S. 1982. Bilingual Competence and Code-mixing in India. *IJOAL*. Vol. 2, No. VIII.

Poplack, S. 1980. Sometimes I'll Start a Sentence in Spanish ... *Linguistics*. 18.

Scotton, C.M., Ury, W. 1977. Bilingual Strategies : The Social Functions of Code-Switching. *Linguistics*. 193.

Shanta, K.M. 1979. Code-Switching : A Study in Bilingual Verbal Strategy. *CIEFL Bulletin*. Vol. 15, No. 1.

Southworth, F.G. 1977. *Functional Aspects of Linguistic Heterogeneity*. In: Sharma and Kumar (eds.).

Sridhar, S.N. 1978. On the Functions of Code-Mixing in Kannada. *International Journal of the Sociology of Language*. 16.

Vaid, J. 1980. The Form and Functions of Code-Mixing in Indian Films : The Case of Hindi and English. *IL*, Vol. 41, No. 1.

Verma, S.K. 1976. Code-Switching : Hindi-English. *Lingua* : 38 : 2

——. 1977. Remarks on *Bilingualism*. In : Sharma and Kumar (Eds.)

Chapter 10

COMMANDS AND REQUESTS IN ENGLISH AND URDU

Though it has been suggested that the difference between commands and requests is one of politeness or courtesy, John Lyons (1977) argues that it may well be that the notion of politeness is inapplicable to commands whereas one can be either polite or impolite in the way in which one makes a request, and an impolite request is not (necessarily) a command. A request, in fact, leaves to the addressee the option of refusal to comply whereas a command does not. Tactfully and politely done, a command takes the shape of a request. Made more tentative it becomes more tactful. A very sure way, as we know, is to use 'please', the well-known term of courtesy. Many languages have special forms of verb, imperatives whose characteristic function is that of use in commands and requests. Admittedly some of the exact communication intention is conveyed by the context and paralinguistic features, but these must be in consonance with the linguistic features themselves'' — (Sirkar, 1978-79).

In both English and Urdu, commands and requests are made according to age, position and status of the person addressed. The 'context of situation' always plays a role. The following are some examples :

Urdu

Command : khiRkiyaN-band karo

Request (simple) : khiRkiyaN-band kar dijiye

Emphatic request : Zara khiRkiyaN-band kar dijiye (toned down)

Insistent request : Zara khiRkiyaN to band kar dijiye

(*to, bhi,* and *hi* are used for stressing something).

English

Commands : Shut the window

Request : Please shut the window

Shut the window, please

Shut the window, if you don't mind.

Polite and implicit commands : The window is open, isn't it?

Official request : Kindly shut the window.

Suggestive command : Shut the window, if you like.

In English, generally speaking, the verb is used before the noun, whereas in Urdu it is placed after the noun. However, as we know, in Urdu expressions as also commands there is no fixed word order. For example, in English we say

Eat the bread.

In Urdu, 'roti khaao' and 'khaao roti' both are used. At the same time, it is also true that 'roti khaao' is the best looking expression though 'khaao roti' does not affect the meaning.

There are certain respectful and polite expressions in Urdu which are used with requests : The following are some of them.

baraah mehrabaani

azraahe mehrabaani

enaayat hogi

nawaazish

baraahe karam

zarra nawaazi.

Platts's (1967 : 458) observation is that when a native scholar of Urdu well acquainted with English is asked to render in Urdu such an expression as 'please (to) do this', he invariably uses the phrase *azraahe mehrabaani isko karo* or *kijiye.* In many cases, however, the phrase 'please to' cannot be applied. *Aap kijiye* is sufficiently honorific and the phrase like *azraahe mehrabaani* is usually dropped in colloquial Urdu.

Hooper (1901 : 49) does not consider *karna* as the infinitive. He argues that the form *na* is gentler and less peremptory than the advisory imperative but asserts that much depends on the niceties of the native feeling. Interestingly, Hooper has made some revealing comparisons between Urdu and English commands. For instance, if what is intended is, as in the English commandment, a prohibition of stealing for all time, then we must say *chori na karna*. Another example is *jo ho so ho mere bete ko wahaN na le jaana* 'whatever happens don't take my son there'.

Both in English and Urdu, the imperative of 'to see' (*dekh, dekho, dekhiye*) is used as an interjection like 'lo', 'behold' and 'see'. Hooper has observed that the native speakers generally do not use any verb but the name or a description of the person addressed in the vocative case e.g., *ai sahib, ai jaanewaale*. If the person seems to be inattentive then *suno* or *suniye* may be used. As in English, unless otherwise marked, the subject of an imperative verb is usually not really expressed and the subject is always a second person pronoun.

Barz (1977 : 61) has noted that it is wrong to think of any of our imperative forms as being intrinsically more polite or less polite than any of the other and that the difference between levels of social relationship has nothing to do with the concept of politeness — we show whether we are polite or impolite by our tone of voice. Often in our usage, the place of 'please' is taken by it. In fact, each of these expressions is equally polite if used in the appropriate social situation. The social stratification found in the imperative reflects the stratification of Indian society. Barz is of the opinion that it is, to be true, a way of making human relationships meaningful and free from anxiety. To cite an example, when a financially well-settled person uses the familiar imperative to a dependent, he is indicating his obligation to that person as a patron as much as he is showing his higher social status. As Barz has emphasized, depending on the sutation, any of our imperative forms could be translated into English with (or without) a 'please'. In general, as we know, our equivalents of 'please' etc. are reserved for more extreme situations. They are formal and not merely polite.

In the matter of tonicity, it is notable that whereas in our language the pattern in commands and requests is generally similar to those in statements in English the tonic is on the last important word :

//ab dhyaan se suno//

//now 'listen càrefully//

Chaswal (1975) finds the same patterns of tonicity in commands, requests and statements.

Both the languages use the interrogative and declarative forms also for issuing commands and making requests.

Talking of the interrogative form, we normally do not use the following form in Urdu :

kya aap darwaaza band kardeNge?

Will you shut the door?

but the following is sometimes heard

Baraah karam darwaaza band kar dijiye.

The form is often used in the negative :

kya aap nahi ayeNge?

In the same way, 'do you mind stopping that?' has no exact equivalent in Urdu. *'kya aap shakkar is taraf barhayeNge*? is not in everyday use. 'Can you possibly give me a lift'? can be said in Urdu as *'kya aap mujhe lift deNge*? The following are some other possible parallels :

English	*Urdu*
Could you lend me your pen?	Kya aap apna qalam mustaar de sakte haiN?
Will you post this letter for me?	Kya aap hamaara khat daal deNge?
Won't you come in and sit down?	Kya aap aakar nahi baetheNge?
Couldn't you possibly come another day?	Kya yeh mumkin nahi ke aap doosre din aayeN?
Would you like to have supper with me?	Kya aap mere saath khaana khaana pasand kareNge?
Can we smoke in here?	Kya ham yehaN cigarette pee sakte haiN.
Are we permitted to smoke in here?	Kya hame yehaN cigarette peene ki ijaazat hai?
Would you mind ...?	aapko khyayaal to nahi hoga or aapko etraaz to nahi hoga.
More coffee?	aur coffee chaahiye? or kya aur leNge?
Will you be quiet?	khaamosh nahi raheNge?

The fact remains, however, that many of these expressions are not frequently heard in informal Urdu. It should also be noted that it is difficult to say 'May I have this dance?' in Urdu. The distinction between 'allowed' and 'permitted' is also difficult to make. 'Can' and 'could', 'will' and 'would' and 'may' and 'might' also cannot be distinguished. 'Pardon', however, can be translated as *maaf kijiye* etc.

In fact, in our idiom we give the effect of 'will', 'would' and 'may' etc. with the help of intonation. 'Have a drink, why don't you'? can be said as *peejiye, kyoN nahi peete*. Though the distinction between polite and not so polite commands in the interrogative is generally not available in Urdu, we get instances of circumlocution.

kya aap darwaaza kholne ki takleef kareNge?

Do you mind opening the door?

But both the yes/no type and wh-type commands are made in Urdu.

The interrogative word 'why' can be rendered in Urdu :

tum yehaN shor kyoN macha rahe ho?
(Why do you make a noise here?)

and also 'how':

tum aisa kaise kahte ho?
(How can you say so?)

At the same time, one finds certain forms of making commands and requests in Urdu which are not available in English.

'A statement+tag question' is always divided into two tone groups in English but the equivalent of it in Urdu *i.e.* the 'na' question is always a single tone group :

//'Buy me a ticket,//won't you?//

// mere ticket khareed deNge na//

If the context is clear enough, even the declarative sentences can serve as a command or request. Perhaps it is not possible to have the 'I wonder' constructions in Urdu. 'Must be' and 'should be' can both be expressed by *chaahiye*. The subtle distinction between 'must' and 'should' is not made in Urdu. The polite expression in English

'I would be extremely grateful if you would write a reference for me' can be put in Urdu in the following way :

Mai bahut mamnoon huNga agar aap mere liye safaarishi khat likh deNge. 'I would be grateful if ...' can be said as *mujhe musarrat hogi agar* ... or *mae shukurguzaar huNga agar* ... or *mae mamnoon huNga agar* ...

'I would appreciate it if ...' is difficult to be rendered in Urdu. 'I am sorry, I didn't quite hear what you said' can be made *maaf kijiye* (or 'farmaaiye') *mae ne suna nahi*. The following are some other possible Urdu equivalents of English commands and requests :

voh shaam me kaam par aa jaayeNge

(They will report for duty in the evening)

jaisa mae kahuN waisa hi kijiye

(You will do exactly as I say)

mae ne unheN khabardaar (or 'agaah') kar diya tha

(I told them they must be careful)

unheN shaam tak Ranchi aana hoga

(He is to return to Ranchi this evening)

tumheN hamaari waapsi tak yehaN thaharna hoga

(You are to stay here until I return)

use waisa karna hoga jaisa mae kahuNga

(He shall do whatever I tell him)

meri darkhaast hae ke voh tanha chali jaye

(I request that she (should) go alone).

Needless to say, one gets things done easily if one tones down one's commands. It is better and more tactful to say to your new secretary.

Would you like to type this letter for me?

or Would you mind typing this letter for me?

As a matter of fact, one can win the confidence of the subordinate more easily by addressing in a tactful way and that is why it is always better to soften our commands. Our students need be told the distinction between 'Will you do this?' and 'would you do this?' Many think that the two expressions are interchangeable ones. They should know the change in the shade of meaning if 'will' is made 'would'. 'Would' indicates a kind of request whereas the use of 'will' makes it more or less a command. Our students should know that there are much softer avenues for giving orders — for example, issuing implicit commands. Also interrogative commands are much more tactful than declarative ones. The use of question tags is another way of lessening the harshness and tenseness of our commands. Intonation plays a vital role in this area and our students should be made conscious of its relevant rules. We should explain to the students clearly that though the subject is avoided in command in both the languages yet in Urdu it is also sometimes used, depending on the context of situation. The frequency of the use of subject in English is very low and if it is inflicted unnecessarily the commands look unnatural. Another important aspect which needs attention in this context is the reported or indirect command.

REFERENCES

Arya, R.C. 1979. "Modality in English and Hindi", CIEFL : Hyderabad : Ph. D. thesis.

Bahri, Hardev 1959. *Hindi Semantics*. Allahabad : Bharati Press.

Barz, R.K. 1977. *An Introduction to Hindi and Urdu*. The Australian National University.

Chaswal, K.K. 1975. "A Comparative Study of the Intonation of English and Hindi" : CIEFL : Research Diploma thesis.

Harley, A.H. 1946. *Colloquial Hindustani*. London : Kegan Paul.

Hooper, D.D. 1901. *Help to the Attainment of Hindustani Idiom*. Christian Literature Society for India.

Leech, G. & Svartvik J. 1975. *Communicative Grammar of English* : Longman.

Lyons, J. 1977. *Semantics*. Cambridge University Press.

Platts, John T. 1967. *A Grammar of the Hindustani or Urdu*. Delhi : Munshiram Manoharlal.

Qurk, Randolph et al. 1972. *Grammar of Contemporary English*.

Sirkar, Arjya. 1978-79. "On Imperatives" *JSL*, Vol. VI, 1 & 2.

Chapter 11

THE USE OF THE PASSIVE IN ENGLISH AND URDU

In modern linguistics, 'voice' refers to the active and passive 'forms' of the verb — it is a grammatical category. It has been said that the opposition of voice in Greek is primarily one of active *vs.* 'middle'. The passive, in fact, developed later and was not in wide use in the age of Latin and Greek literatures.

The passive is of great importance in English. Many have described it as a word-order device since it involves a change in the position and functions of other words in the sentence : it enables us to shift the point of view and to make something topical, thematic and prominent. Generally speaking, the active is agent-oriented and passive goal-oriented. In so far as the form is concerned, the passive is a verbal group consisting of one of the forms of *to be* plus the past participle of a transitive verb. Normally only transitive verbs can be changed from the active to the passive voice. It would not be possible to carry out the active-passive transformation for a sentence that has no complement. The order in a passive sentence is fixed and the passive must come before the main verb. The person or thing that is at the centre of interest at the moment is made the subject of the sentence though it is more natural in English to make the personal object the subject of the passive voice. Of late, there has been a growing tendency to make the indirect object the subject of the passive. At any rate, the main topic is not necessarily indicated by the subject. An active verb + a reflexive pronoun (as in He killed himself) cannot be used when the subject is a thing (*e.g.* "The door opened itself" is not possible). When the reflexive pronoun cannot be deleted the passive voice must be used ('That will be explained' instead of 'That will explain itself'). The agent with 'by' is usually thought to be unnatural in English and is often suppressed and, to be true, most sentences needing it belong rightfully to the active voice. However, the use of the 'agent' in certain contexts becomes unavoidable. Not infrequently, we come across passive constructions with introductory *it.* The passive in English makes use of other verbs besides the verb *to be* such as *get* and *become.*

Admittedly, comparatively much less use is made of the passive in Urdu. The passive in Urdu hardly ever uses the agentive. When the agent is mentioned it is generally advisable to have the verb in the active voice. Of course, the general rule is that the passive should only be used when the agent is not known or when (for a particular consideration) it is thought appropriate to avoid the agent. When it is necessary to mention the agent it is expressed by *ke haath se* or *ki taraf se* or *ki jaanib se* and the instrumental by *se* as *kisi chor ke haathoN chhure se maara gaya* — He was killed by some thief with a dagger. 'He was killed by an elephant' should be converted into *woh haathi ka shikaar ho gaya* or *ek haathi ne use maara.* The action of an agent is described by the use of postposition *se* which, in fact, conveys English 'by'. Generally speaking, some English passive characteristics are available in Urdu 'majhul' constructions. Possibly, the very distinction of the passive has been borrowed from English. This category, otherwise, was perhaps not present in its present form in the Urdu grammar — except, of course, in the case of 'majhul' verb where the agent is not known. Significantly, the equivalences of English active/passive sentences *e.g.,*

mae ne khat likha

khat mujh se likha gaya

are not in equally wide use in Urdu. The first is a recognised Urdu usage but the second, though perhaps not ungrammatical, is against the very temperament of the Urdu language. Maybe this is a plain imitation of English and, strictly speaking, if we are allowed to say so, is not Urdu at all. The few passive constructions of this nature which we come across in Urdu have been possibly directly borrowed from and are in imitation of the English syntax. Most books of Urdu grammar now, however, take note of this category. "The English construction 'I am beaten' becomes in Urdu 'I go beaten'. The latter is called the passive voice" — Rahman (1965 : 119). Here 'go' (*gaya*) indicates the temporal movement and not the spatial *i.e.* the act of my being beaten has come to an end.

The passive is formed in Urdu by conjugating the past participle of a transitive or a causal verb with appropriate forms of the verb *jaana* as *maara jaana.* The participle though carried throughout the entire conjugation is not unaffected by the gender and the number of the subject. The following changes are made to conform to the gender :

woh maara gaya He was killed.

woh maare gaye They were killed.

woh maari gayi She was killed.

Pushpa, Sushma aur Veena maari gayiN : Pushpa, Sushma and Veena were killed. Though the subject of the passive is usually in the nominative, it is often in modern Urdu put in the accusative :

uska qatl kiya gaya.

Though the above construction is widely acceptable in Urdu it makes students go wrong in English :

His/him was killed.

The grammatical form in Urdu will be :

woh qatl kiya gaya — He was killed.

The passive is idiomatically used in Urdu to describe possibility or impossibility either of moral or physical nature *e.g.,*

qismat se laRa nahi jaata — One cannot contend with fate.

mujh se laRa nahi jaata — I cannot fight.

Thus we can say that the passive voice with a proper agent expressed (in Urdu) 'I could not bear to' — or 'I was unable to' *e.g.,*

mujh se dushman ke saamne jaaya na gaya :

mujh se uski shikayat na dekhi gayi.

Talking of the participles, *dekha jaata* is used for the present and is found only in finite terms while *dekha gaya* indicates the past. It should be remembered that the ordinary past participle — *dekha, dekha hua* — seen (feminine : *dekhi, dekhi hui*) is also passive just as the corresponding participle in English. The past participle of a transitive verb is always passive (Bailey : 1974 : 54). In Urdu many kinds of transitive verbs made up of two or more words can be used in the passive voice. For example :

(i) Compound verbs e.g., *dena, lena, daalna, rakhna* as their second element

(ii) Verbs made of noun or adjective and verb :

radio mol liya gaya — The radio was bought.

(iii) *lagna, sakna,* and *chukna* can be used along with the passive :

joRa siya jaa chuka — The suit of clothes has been sewn.

(iv) Verbs used in constructions giving expression to necessity, duty etc. :

us waqt report likhi jaani thi — At that time a report had to be written.

(v) Along with *rahna* and the present participle showing continuity:

paaejame siye jaate raheNge The trousers will continue being made.

(vi) Two verbs used together as a form of repetition :

wahiN paala posa gaya It was there he was brought up and looked after.

(vii) A very characteristic use is the impersonal passive with the logical nominative governed by *ko*, which means 'as for' or 'with regard to' etc.

us ko bartaraf kar diya gaya — He was dismissed.

The straightforward passive is also used :

woh bartaraf kiya gaya — He was dismissed.

(viii) The negative passive expresses inability.

cannot, could not etc.

Kachru (1965 : 181) has stressed that one of the constituent elements of the Aux. is the passive marker ya+jaa and a sentence of the form

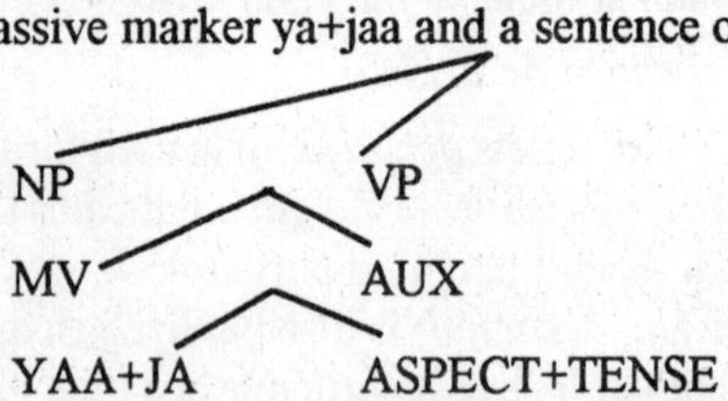

is a passive sentence. The passive marker ya+ja has a capabilitative meaning also. For example, the sentence *Zaid se khat nahi likha gaya* means either 'Zaid could not write a letter' or 'The letter was not written by Zaid'. The passives of V_i sentences have a capabilitative meaning : and, notably, agentives are used in such sentences and they may come as theme also :

Zaid se thakaavat ke maare chala nahi gaya

'Zaid' 'by' 'fatigue' 'owing to' 'was not walked'.

'Zaid was not capable of walking as he was too tired'.

The passives of V_t also have meaning of this nature. For instance,

Zaid se motor nahi kharidi gayi

'Zaid' 'buy' 'motor' 'not' 'was bought'

Zaid was not capable of buying a motor.

Yeh bojh saha nahi jaata

This burden is intolerable.

Zaid kitaabeN bechta hae is the present indefinite active ($NP_1 + NP_2 + V_t$ + hae) of which the passive will be *kitaabeN bechi jaati haeN* ($NP_2 + V_t$ + jaati haeN) — Books are sold (some people might insist on retaining the agent here). An example of the active in the present continuous tense in Urdu is *woh naqshe bana rahe haeN* ($NP_1 + NP_2 + V_t$ + rahe haeN) of which the passive form will be *naqshe banaaye jaa rahe haeN* ($NP_2 + V_t$ + ja + rahe haeN)— pictures are being drawn. It should be noted here that 'bech' is the root to which the perfective aspect *a* or *ee* is added. *jaa* is the active verb aspect to which *ti hae* of passive is added. In much the same way, *banaaya* is the active verb aspect to which *jaa raha hae* or *jaa rahe haeN* is added. The normal construction of the passive can be illustrated as follows : NP se NP (vp V AUX) where V is a perfective participle. Often, however, a pronoun in the passive subject tends to be preposed to the head of the sentence :

Voh dushman se maare jayeNge

They will be killed by the enemy. (Imai : 1979).

As has already been pointed out, far less use is made of the passive in Urdu than in English. Hooper is of the view that the reason is that passivization implies a free agent and the Indian mind is so saturated with pantheistic philosophy that though there is much in language which implies a practical belief in free agency yet the tendency, in general, is to avoid the expression of it. Hooper has emphasized that when in English the passive voice is used, Urdu uses instead the simple root form of the verb, when the latter is intransitive in meaning *e.g.*,

This table is well made

yeh mez achhi bani hae or *bangayi hae*

'this' 'table' has well come into made state.

To a native speaker of English the primary idea is 'to make' as a voluntary act, and 'to be made' is a secondary idea, as being the product of the former, the result of the voluntary action. To the speaker of Urdu, as has been noted by Hooper, the main thought is that the table has come out of an unmade state into a made one; and the further thought that someone has effected this transformation, is a secondary one; and the still further thought that the transformation has been effected through free agency, is so far removed from their habits of thinking that they seek to avoid having to express it. Similarly, "no corn is sold in this market" would be *is bazaar meN anaj* not *becha nahi jaata* but *nahi bikta.*

Another reason for the rather infrequent use of the passive in Urdu is that alternative forms are available. As for example, the existence of neuter verbs in Indian languages also account for the sparing use of the passive. These neuter verbs are passive in form but active in meaning *e.g.,*

Yeh kapRa kahaN banta hae

Where is this cloth made?

A convenient way of avoiding the passive in Urdu is to turn it into active and make the agent the subject of the verb. It would be appropriate to say *us waqt rooh yasoo ko le gayi* in Urdu (the active form) for 'Then was Jesus led up by the spirits'. Sometimes the third person plural active is preferred to the passive e.g., *kahte haeN* — 'they say' or 'it is said'. Instead of the passive, other idiomatic expressions in Urdu are — an intransitive verb, simple or compund e.g., *pitna* to be beaten — an Arabic or Persian past participle e.g., *malum hua* — to be known — a transitive verb with an object — *maar khaana* — to be beaten — literally 'to eat strokes' — *shikast khaana* or *paana* — to be defeated — *tawajjah dilaana* — to draw attention.

The mechanism of passivization in Urdu is different from that of English in a marked way. In Urdu passive constructions are marked by a nominal group as agentive and a verb in its perfective aspect followed by 'jaa' as component of the verbal group at predicate. As against English, the agentive nominal group in Urdu, as many say, occupies clause position. Both in English and Urdu, the passive verb is marked by the verb *to be* which is followed by the lexical or main verb in its past participle form (*i.e.* to be + V^{en}). In English the word order is fixed whereas in Urdu it is less so and sentences like 'John eats fish' can be written in any of the permutations without considerably affecting the meaning.

We have many instances where double transitives have the potentialities of two passive transformations. Significantly, in Urdu it is restricted to only one. Apparently, the Urdu speakers find it difficult to convert the explicit agent into passive, although verb change is more or less the same. Generally, a sentence in Urdu, where the agent is to be mentioned, gets active form. In the passive constructions the agent will be almost invariably deleted. In English only recoverable agents are dropped. Therefore, generally speaking, agentives cannot be translated into Urdu where we find (more or less) agentless passive, *e.g.*,

The Irani students have released the American hostages.

Irani tolaba ne Amriki qaidiyoN ko raha kar diya hae.

The American hostages have been released by the Irani students

Amriki qaidi raha kar diye gaye haeN.

It is difficult to use the agentive here. Alternatives like :

Amriki qaidi Irani tolaba ki haraasat se raha kiye gaye

or

Amriki qaidi Irani tolaba ki taraf se raha kar diye gaye
ki jaanib se
ke zariye

are not appropriate ones. It is really very difficult to find exact passive equivalents and that is why agentives are often omitted. Also, many things cannot be said in the passive. At the same time, there are many passive patterns in English without any passive counterparts in Urdu. In respect of the pseudo-passive also it is difficult to get the active counterpart. In such constructions, as :

mujh se yeh kaam nahi ho sakta

agentives can be used and *se* will come with them. It will not be out of place to mention here that *hemingway ki likhi hui* and *dhobi ka dhoya hua kapRa* are instances of adjectival phrase.

The passive in Urdu is different from that in English both in construction and in usage and it is not at all as widespread as in English. The use of the passive in English and Urdu is not interchangeable either. In fact, grammatical equivalents of all categories of the passive in English are not available in Urdu usage. But Urdu has several other alternative idiomatic expressions. The passive is idiomatically used in Urdu to describe capability (*mujh se khaana nahi khaaya jaata*), possibility or impossibility etc. The word-order in Urdu is less fixed. In the Urdu passive the agent is generally not retained.

REFERENCES

Bailey, T. Graham, 1974. *Urdu, Teach Yourself Books.*

Harley, A.H. 1946. *Colloquial Hindustani*, London : Kegan Paul.

Hooper, D.D. 1901. *Help to the Attainment of Hindustani Idiom.* Christian Literature Society of India.

Imai, Takashi. 1979. ''On Impersonal Passive in Hindi. *IL*, Volume 40, No. 2.

Kachru, Y. 1965. *An Introduction to Hindi Syntax.* University of Illinois.

Kellog, S.H. 1876. *A Grammar of the Hindi Language.* London : Kegan Paul.

Lyons, J. 1974. *Introduction to Theoretical Linguistics.*

Phillot, D.C. 1918. *Hindustani Manual.* Calcutta.

Rahman, Azizur, 1965. *Teach Yourself Urdu.* Karachi : Aziz's Oriental Book Depot.

Scholeberg, H.C. 1950. *Concise Grammar of the Hindi Language*. London : OUP.

Chapter 12

PROGRESSIVE POETRY AND PROPAGANDA

Prof. Kalimuddin Ahmad's Criticism on Progressive Urdu Poetry

The movement of the progressive writers in Urdu was begun around 1930 when the nationalist movement in literature was undergoing a radical change. The movement was formally started in Urdu under the leadership of Sajjad Zaheer, Dr. Abdul Alim and others. Tagore, Nehru, Premchand and Maulvi Abdul Haque were among those who blessed and encouraged the new movement. There is no denying the fact that almost all the branches of literature were energized and activated by this movement. But, with the passage of time, as the hold of Marxism on this literary movement grew stronger, the dull purposefulness characteristic of it also increased and, as a matter of fact, 'art' was virtually sacrificed at the altar of 'message'. All this eventually led to a stage where apparently mere slogan shouting reigned supreme. Much that was thus produced was probably devoid of literary and creative beauty. It was generally difficult to raise a finger against this kind of literature since almost all powerful literary critics were themselves progressives. In an atmosphere where hardly anybody could open his lips against progressive writers Prof. Kalimuddin Ahmad stood up against this storm firmly and tried, not without success, to break the idols in this temple.

Prof. Ahmad's criticism on progressive poetry has been scathing and Dr. Ahsan Faruqi thinks that Prof. Ahmad was most suited to pass judgments on this issue because of his sound knowledge of and remarkable insight into western literature. Prof. Ahmad divides the progressive movement into two sections. On the one side are the views which the progressive writers try to propagate and on the other is the literature which is produced bearing in mind these basic principles. To Prof. Ahmad this literature is absolutely unsatisfying. He advances two reasons for the failure of this literature : the principles and assumptions on which this literature is founded and on which these writers base their arguments are exposed to criticism and also, generally, this literature is devoid of vital literary qualities. Prof. Ahmad concludes that this may be anything but literature. He does not like the progressives since they give undue importance to theme at the cost of style (Dr. Khalilurrahman Azmi is also of this opinion) and their style, as he observes, lacks finish and individuality. Majaz's similes have been found inappropriate and vague and he has been mentioned as merely playing with words (as Josh also does). Prof. Ahmad is of the view that the progressives failed to throw overboard the unprofitable legacies of earlier Urdu poetry *e.g.*, a variety of unnecessary details, characteristic of leisurely poetry, a habitual repetition as a feature of style, a continued use of the Ghazal style which had almost exhausted its possibilities and extravagance in the use of words. He makes two exceptions in this context – Firaq and Faiz. He finds that Faiz fulfils the artistic requirements of poetry and also maintains a kind of self-control *i.e.* Faiz avoids slogan shouting. Unlike Majaz he does not give overmuch value to his adolescent experience. It is in Faiz's poem *Tanhaai* that, according to Prof. Ahmad, the Urdu 'nazm' gets rid of the 'ghazal'. These poets, in fact, wrote both nazms and ghazals and they claim that they have brought about changes and developments in ghazal-writing. Prof. Ahmad does not agree with them and does not find any mark of distinction, any sign of development in their ghazals from the point of view of technique. It is true that the same cannot be said about the themes of their ghazals where the boundaries have been definitely extended by them though the same themes are to be found in their nazms as well. Just like the traditional ghazal, the world of the progressive ghazal does not acquire a breadth even thematically. Simply, old vocabulary and phraseology (as Prof. Ahmad accuses) have given place to new. Perhaps the progressives do all this because they are, in the opinion of Prof. Ahmad, inherently romantics. Rebellion, labour, hydrogen-bomb, peace and dollar etc. are the new themes that the progressives have brought with them to the realm of ghazal. The repetition of the same themes oratorically leaves a bad taste in the mouth. He asserts that these writers just fail to become literateurs particularly because they do not choose their words carefully.

Prof. Ahmad quotes the sympathisers of the progressive literature copiously and finds the predominance in this literature of some communist thoughts (and, in the opinion of Prof. Ahmad, the progressives give overmuch significance to the thought element). Progressives, according to him, give undue importance to the views of the politicians and economists and try to give a literary colour to their thoughts (and also try to give the impression that the thoughts are their own). Prof. Ahmad remarks that every progressive goes to the same fountain-head (*i.e.* Marxism) and no one is prepared to undergo the rigours of finding out a fresh fountain. In Prof. Ahmad's words, as the progressives desire to propagate the views of others they are no better than brokers or agents who sell the goods actually obtained from others and since the ideas are borrowed Prof. Ahmad sees no reason why credit should be given to the agents when one can get to the origins. Consequently, now the only thing to be analysed, as he says, is 'how' the thing has been said. Unfortunately, he asserts, to this aspect these writers do not pay any attention at all. Indisputably, if the thing is well said propaganda can also become literature. To the progressives symbols are unnecessary and that is why they prefer saying things directly. According to Prof. Ahmad, the poetry of the progressives generally is not very far from prose though, now and then, as he admits, even their propaganda becomes real literature.

Marx, Engels and Lenin, in fact, belong to the domains of economics and politics. They have laid the foundations of communist economy and communist form of government. All this is undeniable but the question posed here by Prof. Ahmad is as to how they creep into the world of creative literature. Marx gave considerable significance to literature : he took literature on the one hand to be a social document or report and on the other a tool to educate the masses with. Certainly, Marx knew how to use literature in the service of a revolution. But, as one would expect, Prof. Ahmad asks whether literature written for a certain purpose and not impartially is literature in the strict sense. To him obvious slogan shouting and political propaganda are not genuine literature. It is the Marxist philosophy (the roots of which Prof. Ahmad finds hollow since, as he points out, Marx based his philosophy on a very weak one propounded by Hegel) which, as he remarks, every progressive writer considers his first duty to go on repeating. The effect of such writing (wherein the society is beaten with a Marxist stick), if any, will be only a temporary and time-serving one : these writers, to be very true, are not free agents since all the time they are frightened of their 'comrades' in the party and they have to toe the party-line in any case. These writers do not realise (Prof. Ahmad asserts) that there is no harm if they do not mention 'Inqilab' (revolution) again and again. Naturally, as he says, 'Inqilab' cannot be achieved merely by chanting the word. Thus in the ultimate analysis such poetry comes to mere shouting slogans, pure and simple, and there is a clear lack of depth of emotion and thought. Prof. Ahmad accuses the progressives of making a 'criminal' attempt to inject economics into the already anaemic body of Urdu literature. These progressives appear to him better conversant with communism than with literature itself. They seek inspiration from only those western writers in whose writings communism gets the upper hand since they were so fully enveloped in communist thoughts as to be unable to contemplate on any issue in a detached manner : progressivism to Prof. Ahmad is just another name for Marxism. He is perhaps unwilling to let economics etc. enter the world of literature. Prof. Ahmad here appears to be at one with another critic who says that when propaganda enters from one door literature makes good its escape from the other.

Though Prof. Ahmad speaks approvingly of some practical aspects of communism he makes disparaging criticism of its outlook. At times, however, the progressives receive bouqets from him when he admits that they have brought poetry and life closer to each other. Nevertheless, he is not going to allow poets to participate in any movement directly and the partcipation, as he feels, does not necessarily make one a better poet either. He feels that it is not the duty of a poet to present the merits of communism and demerits of capitalism or for that matter anything else.

It is perhaps not wholly justified to take the progressives to task simply because they have gone to Marx, Engels, Lenin or any other person for thoughts and feelings: W.L. Phelps has observed, 'All great poets have the power of indignation, a divine wrath against wickedness in high places. The poets, like the prophets of old, pour out their irrepressible fury against what they believe to be cruelty and oppression. Milton's magnificent Piedmont sonnet is a glorious roar of righteous rage; and since his time the poets have ever been the spokesmen for the insulted and injured ... I do not know what humanity would do without its poets – they are the artificial conventions of society.' Though I do not say that the progressives under discussion stand any comparison with Milton the fact remains that such writings also have a significance which cannot be underrated : they play a conspicuous role in upholding an ideal.

Undoubtedly, these poets took a keen interest in political issues and were also largely concerned with social problems. Prof. Ahmad remarks, however, that perhaps some of our progressives are aware of politics and economics but they are definitely not in touch with other branches of knowledge like history, anthropology, psychology, and fine arts etc.

Politics has never been a bed of roses even for politicians. For a poet to enter into this realm would be extremely risky. Such a poet makes enemies and critics condemn him and, sometimes, go to the extent of denying him even his very title — the title of being a poet. It is true, to a large extent, that such a poet is a loser, so to say, in many respects and he is often swamped by attacks denouncing his lack of emotion, passion and genuine inspiration. It is often said that the intellectual element gets the upper hand in his poetry. Sometimes he is dismissed only as a political orator. It should be stressed here, however, that politics is obviously not a forbidden fruit for the poet.[1] For instance, politics has never been alien to English literature. Shakespeare emphasized the significance of justice as the base of true power and Milton preached the importance of liberty to the individual. Wordsworth is often considered to be the first poet to claim authority for the poet to meddle with social affairs.

Great literature combines both realism and idealism and literature has always been a vehicle of social criticism, It is true that one cannot exist without bread and it is equally true that without it one cannot create literature. But, is it all that one requires? If a person gets many loaves of bread does it necessarily mean that he would start pouring forth great literature? Naturally, there are a number of other things that make one a poet. Prof. Ahmad notes that literature is directly related to mind and thus the mind is more important than the belly : man's most vital requirements are the satisfaction of mental desires and development of mental powers rather than the loaves of bread. The period during which these progressives thrived was politically and economically an eventful one and obviously it was not possible for them to remain immune to whatever was happening around. We might not agree with all their views but, once again, agreement is not a necessary condition for the enjoyment of poetry. Even in English the neo-realists in post-Second World War poetry tend to incite revolt and write about purely economic problems, though their output has been often dismissed as 'too sordid' and 'too materialistic idealism'.

F.R. Leavis, who has had considerable influence on Prof. Ahmad, considers Marxist approach to literature 'unprofitable' though he concedes that literature is not a matter of isolated works of art, belonging to a realm of pure literary values. It is evident that contemporary social situation will be reflected in literary works. We are in complete agreement with Prof. Ahmad when he lays emphasis on genuine inspiration and passion in the poet. If a poet intends to deal with social problems he must possess alongwith the practical acumen of the statesman the imagination and the sympathy of the poet : he should have enough of creative ability, too. But the question that arises here is whether the progressive poets lack these elements completely. Perhaps this stand is not fully justified. Admittedly, there have been moments in the careers of some of these poets when they have shown that they are not wholly devoid of these elements. One opinion is that propaganda or the desire to plead for a particular cause is by itself a legitimate source of inspiration. All said and done, Prof. Ahmad is fairly correct when he shows that not many of the progressives have succeeded (to an appreciable degree) in taming the propagandist in them. The poet who chooses political and social themes as his normal source of inspiration is not to be held up to ridicule, but, at the same time, the sociologist must not get the better of the artist. It appears that themes have overpowered many of these poets leaving poetry simply an intellectual exercise, thus reducing their writings to just prosaic statements. Consequently, many a time one feels that their social and political convictions have seized the throne (which is not permissible in the realm of art). That is why, Prof. Ahmad thinks that these progressives do not sincerely strive to become 'poets' *i.e.* they do not try to acquire poetic qualities. He feels that whatever they do (for example, when they shout slogans for peace or for war) they murder poetry all the same.

Ali Sardar Jafri receives brickbats from him because, in his opinion, Jafri finds the entire world in the dark room of Marxism. According to Prof. Ahmad, Jafri made a conscious attempt to make literature a weapon of social struggle for the good of the masses. When Jafri suppresses the orator in him and restricts himself to the traditional limits he writes good poetry but, like Josh, he, too, believes in overdoing the descriptions (which irritates a fine sensibility). Prof. Ahmad observes that Firaq also gives publicity to Marxist viewpoints and that Marxism has coloured all his thoughts. Majaz's poetry has also been found to be based chiefly on Marxist thoughts and, as a result, his experiences have been described as raw and adolescent.

Prof. Ahmad is unhappy with the progressives because they have been influenced more by Marxist thoughts and less by the Russian language and literature and because they do not understand that poetry is something universal and is not the sole property of a certain class or group. There is no quarrelling with them if they want to destroy capitalism and install communism in its place. But Prof. Ahmad finds fault with the means they adopt, one of them being poetry. What he actually wanted from the progressives, however, was an honest declaration that they would use poetry for a purpose and that rhetoric and propaganda would be the special features of this poetry, because that was the need of the hour. Poetry has its basis, Prof. Ahmad goes on to explain, in valuable human experiences and experiences of this nature cannot be associated with a particular 'time', 'group' or 'objective'. The experiences of this type are not likely to cease to exist even when communism is established in the whole world. According to Prof. Ahmad the progressive poets are so much preoccupied with this particular objective that they dismiss everything that does not have revolutionary reverberations or communist colouring in it.

We find that a substantial part of the progressive poetry has been lost sight of as the themes were mostly ephemeral. The progressive poetry, as Prof. Ahmad has said, often did not possess many of those virtues which go to make great poetry. But, at least, during the early stages of this movement some of these writers wrote with remarkable moderation. It is also true that progressive poetry in Urdu has a number of achievements to its credit and, in fact, there is no dearth of genuine creative poets. Thus, perhaps, Prof. Ahmad's criticism on progressive poetry written in Urdu has been produced with predilection since he has preferred to ignore the merits of this poetry completely.

NOTES

1. 'Group loyalties are necessary, and yet they are poisonous to literature, so long as literature is the product of individuals. As soon as they are allowed to have any influence, even a negative one on creative writings, the result is not only falsification, but often the actual drying-up of the inventive faculties...

   'Do we have to conclude that it is the duty of every writer to "keep out of politics"? Certainly not ... and he should be able to act cooperatively while if he chooses, completely rejecting the official ideology ...

   'But does all this mean ... that he (the writer) would refrain from writing about politics? One again, certainly not. There is no reason why he should not write in the most crudely political way, if he wishes to : only he should do so as an individual, an outsider, at the most an unwelcome guerilla on the flank of a regular army. This attitude is quite compatible with ordinary political usefulness.

   "In our time it is broadly true that political writing is bad writing. Where it is not true, it will generally be found that the writer is some kind of rebel, expressing his private opinions and not a 'party-line'."

George Orwell

REFERENCES

Ahmad, Kalimuddin, *Amli Tanqeed* (1963).

——, *Urdu Shaeri par Ek Nazar* (1966).

——, *Sokhanhai Guftani* (1967).

——, *Urdu Tanqeed par Ek Nazar* (1969).

Alam, Qaiser Zoha, "The Mind and Art of Sir William Watson", unpublished Ph.D. thesis, Ranchi University (1967).

Azmi, Khalilurrahman, *Urdu Me Taraqqi Pasand Adabi Tahreek* (1972).

Faruqi, Ahsan, *Urdu Me Tanqeed* (year not mentioned).

Leavis, F.R., *The Common Pursuit* (1952).

Orwell, George, *Collected Essays* (1961).

Phelps, W.L., *The Advance of English Poetry in the Twentieth Century* (1938).

Selincourt, E. de, *English Poetry and the National Ideal* (1915).

Chapter 13

IQBAL, THE SATIRIST

Sir Sheikh Abdul Qadir was of the opinion that in Iqbal Ghalib had taken a re-birth. In a re-assessment, Professor Asloob Ahmed Ansari has placed Iqbal among the world's greatest poets. Professor Ansari has observed that in certain areas Iqbal's significance is even greater than Ghalib's as a poet. Shamsurrahman Faruqi has (recently) emphasised Iqbal's greatness as a poet (as distinguished from Iqbal — the philosopher or Iqbal — the reformer, etc.). Iqbal's poems have been translated into all important languages of the world and, of late, much interest has been taken in them in Arab countries. Iqbal's impact on language has been remarkable and his experiments with the form of poetry have been considered interesting and valuable.

Iqbal's poetry is indeed an exquisite blend of religion, art and thought. Undoubtedly Iqbal has many things in common with Ghalib — both upheld the dignity of man. If Ghalib went to the extent of saying:

Even though a servant I am free and proud
I shall come back if the gate of the kaaba is not wide open.

Iqbal also did not lag behind :

Rise thy self to such a height that before the approaching destiny
God should ask man, "What dost thou desire?"

He has repeatedly addressed God with a rebel-like approach. He protested (in *Shikwah*) against God's complacent and careless attitude:

Yet there is a complaint that we are not faithful;
If we are not faithful, Thou art not beloved as well.

In *Sawal* a self-respecting poor man has absolutely no grievance regarding his poverty but he prays to God to let him know whether certain fools have acquired riches with God's permission. Though Iqbal's was a voice of dissent he was all humility. William Watson, a late-Victorian English poet, comes to mind. Watson protested against God's treatment of man and put forth the case of human dignity and man's indispensability. It may be interesting to compare the two poets though in *Shikwah* Iqbal talked chiefly about Muslims. We must remember that Iqbal and Watson, living in different hemispheres, were contemporaries.

It has been said that the subject of Iqbal's poetry is man:

Love of humanity is a soul-nourishing wine
This thing has taught me to be inebriated sans cup.

He shed tears as he found trouble and strife everywhere and was taken aback at violence and bloodshed. Iqbal's message is one of universal brotherhood and international friendship. It is said about Tagore that Bengal was simply the medium through which he actually gave a message to the entire humanity. The same can be said, with some reservations, about references to Muslims as found in Iqbal's poetry.

Iqbal's love and sympathy for the downtrodden was undoubted and unbounded. He has, therefore, denounced exploitation in no uncertain terms. He himself led the life of a *dervish*. His concern with the life of the individual in society and his problems in a highly organised social system has been particularly taken note of by his critics. His work deals with aspects of human life in terms of the doctrine of Self and the immortality of the soul:

It never faces defeat;
It passes out of sight but never perishes.

Anwar Beg notes that it is as a humanist that Iqbal will be specially remembered by the posterity as he was one of the few idealists of the contemporary world who never lost touch with reality. Iqbal 'laid great emphasis on the independence of man in his approach towards life'.

Iqbal wrote at length on the greatness of man. He placed humanity at a very high level and nothing can come close by. In his poem, *God and Man*, God addressed man and said that He gave many amenities which could have been further developed by man with his strength and intellect but man has, in fact, made things worse. Man refutes this charge vehemently by saying that he was blessed with only raw and unfinished materials which he has converted, to the best of his ability, into commodities of utility.

Kurmali phonology, it is interesting to note, does not possess consonant clusters though abutting consonants are often heard *i.e.* 'a sequence of consonants which extends over two syllables' (Abercrombie: 1967: 76). We define here consonant clusters in relation to the structure of the syllable and we make a distinction between a cluster and a sequence of abutting consonants. Thus the sequence /sl/ in *slate* is a cluster but not in *misled*, where it consists of abutting consonants – /s/ arresting the first syllable and /1/ releasing the second. Kurmali speakers (like many people) find the sequence /sl/ difficult as a cluster but pronounce it easily when it occurs as a sequence of abutting consonants. It should be pointed out here that these tribal languages of the area have Mundari as their guardian and, as a trait, all the languages are without consonant clusters. Naturally, therefore, when they use an English word containing a consonant cluster they modify the pronunciation accordingly. We will cite some examples of this kind — English words with consonant clusters used in Kurmali in a modified form. Kurmali speakers use various devices to make up for the absence of the consonant cluster in their phonology. We do, however, come across a cluster in Kurmali speech when they pronounce 'tube' as 'tue', if we take the semivowel /j/ as a consonant. Syllabic consonants have also been considered here as parts of clusters (Cohen : 1965) though syllabic elements function like vowels in the structure of the syllable in which they occur.

One of the devices that Kurmali speakers use with a view to avoiding the cluster is slurring or often even elision — when they drop a phoneme altogether *e.g.*, we find two changes when the word 'station' is made 'tesan' in Kurmali:

(i) the initial /s/ has been dropped because it formed a cluster with /t/ (ii) /š/has been made /s/ — /š/ is also not found in Kurmali phonology. Interestingly, the word 'station' is pronounced 'tesan' or 'teesan' also by uneducated people who speak other languages as mother tongue in this area as also in other parts of Bihar.

The /p/ of the cluster /p1/ is dropped completely when 'platform' is made 'latfaram'. Perhaps 'p' of the cluster 'pl' is dropped because of the sound in the later part of the word as 'pl' in 'plate' restrains 'p' and the word is pronounced as 'pelet' – a vowel sound is inserted between the two consonants. 'Lantern' is made 'lalten'. Here again /r/ (which is audibly pronounced in Indian English) is dropped to enable the speaker to utter the word without the cluster. Almost the same goes for the following words:

trolly	—	tali
driver	—	diver
transfer	—	tenesfer
permanent	—	parmenti
result	—	rejel

The device that Kurmali speakers often adopt during their use of English words containing consonant clusters is that of epenthesis *i.e.* insertion of one or more sounds into loan words to make them conform to the phonological pattern of the borrowing language. We find instances of prothesis *i.e.* inserting a vowel initially before the cluster or of anaptyxis *i.e.* medially between the two consonants or even finally *i.e.* after the cluster. Initially, for exammple :

screw	—	iskulup
school	—	iskul
scholarship	—	iskalarsip

What we find in the above three cases is in fact almost a pan-Indian feature — introducing a short prothetic vowel before the cluster and thus dividing the cluster into parts of two different syllables.

A vowel is frequently introduced in between the two consonants of the cluster. As a result, monosyllables are often split into two syllables. This tendency is to be found in the speakers of many other North Indian languages as well. For example, instead of saying 'glass' they say 'gilas' (because, as we know, they find consonant cluster difficult). Other relevant instances borrowed from Kurmali are the following:

slate	—	silat	
slipper	—	silpat	
handle	—	hendel	(a sequence of abutting consonants)
class	—	kilas	(")
electric	—	elektiri	
farm	—	faram	
plate	—	pelet	
brush	—	burus	
drum	—	daram	
brake	—	berek	
blade	—	beled	
frame	—	ferem	
button	—	batan	
charge	—	charaj	
frock	—	farak	(")

captain	—	kepten
flute	—	fulut
settle	—	setel
film	—	filim
chance	—	chanas
torch	—	tarach

The addition of a vowel medially — in between the two consonants of a cluster *i.e.* anaptyxis, is not exclusive to Kurmali. In fact, 'farm' becomes 'faram' in the spoken language of many not-so-educated people in Bihar with different linguistic backgrounds. When in Kurmali 'cement' is pronounced as 'sirmit', 'jail' as 'jehal' and 'daylight' as 'derlight', epenthetic consonants and not vowels are introduced. When 'inspector' becomes 'nispitar' in Kurmali, the initial /i/ is dropped and a vowel phoneme is introduced between the consonants *i.e.* /n/ and /s/. Also, the consonant /k/ is omitted.

As is clear from a number of examples cited above, often Kurmali speakers split a monosyllable with a cluster into a disyllable. This phenomenon becomes very interesting when they insert a phoneme or even a syllable finally in order to avoid the cluster. For example, 'lamp' which contains a cluster in the final position is converted into 'lamfo'. The following are other instances :

pant	—	pentul
box	—	baska
bolt	—	voltu
kettle	—	ketli
mantle	—	menthen
first	—	fasto

When using English words Kurmali speakers tend to convert, though not always, the phoneme /n/ before /t/ into /l/ *e.g.*:

fountain	—	falten
lantern	—	lalten

It is worth mentioning here, however, that alternative pronunications are also noticed. 'Fanten' is also occasionally heard. The word 'manager' gets only a vowel mutation and becomes 'munijar'. 'Doctor' is made both 'dagdar' and 'daktar'. /d/ becomes /t/ in 'petal' (for 'pedal') and 'contector' (for 'conductor'). Let it be mentioned here that the sound /z/ is also not present in their phonology. Certain English words when used in Kurmali undergo major phonetic changes.

To cite a few examples:

freewheel	—	ferul
slipper	—	silpat
cement	—	sirmit
screw	—	iskulup
cork	—	kag
retired	—	retan

'Line' becomes 'nael' which is perhaps an instance of metathesis — almost an interchange of phonemes. When 'settle' becomes 'setel' and means 'practice' in Kurmali it is a case of semantic change — one of shift or transfer of sense — though clearly the word is borrowed from English. Sometimes certain words are pronounced with a r (or R) sound *e.g.*, 'third' is 'thaR' and 'record' is 'rakeR'. In fact rd becomes R. Many Indian languages including Urdu have converted the ancient Prakrit Sanskrit 'jade' into 'jaRa' and the middle Prakrit 'ghodo', 'ghado', 'kadaho' and 'kapdo' into 'ghoRa', 'ghaRa', 'kaRahi' and 'kapRa' respectively (Sabzwari: 1975: 27).

In many of these borrowings the influence of Hindi is apparent — they have often been adopted the way the Hindi speakers (particularly the uneducated ones) use them. To mention a few clear cases :

jail	—	jehal	
sweater	—	suitar	
barrister	—	balester	
office	—	afis	
verandah	—	beramda	
tarpaulin	—	tirpal	
signal	—	sengal	(another instance of metathesis)
kerosene	—	kerasin	
tyre	—	tayar	
gear	—	geyar	

The /r/ sound after a vowel often tends to become /l/ as in 'balester' and 'karnel' (for 'corner'). The short 'a' sound often becomes 'u' (perhaps to facilitate vowel harmony) :

company	—	kumpani
compounder	—	kumpaunder

Whereas 'o' sometimes become 'a' *e.g.* :

support — sapat

In fact, these vowel mutations appear interesting though they are often wayword. The vowel /æ/ repeatedly becomes /e/, *e.g.* :

matric — metric
captain — kepten
battery — betri
balloon — belun

As a matter of fact, the diphthongs are often made monophthongs *e.g.*, 'plate' becomes 'pelet'. At the same time, frequently the short vowels are changed into long vowels *e.g.*, :

cup — kap
question — kaschen
circus — sarkes.

In spite of the Bengali influence, the rounded vowels /)/ and /):/ are often changed into unrounded ones. For instance:

torch — tarach
platform — latfaram
frock — farak
scholarship — iskalarsip

Some other interesting examples of the changes undergone by the English words when used by Kurmali speakers are the following :

carrier — kariat
ring — rim
ticket — tikis
hospital — haspatal
tube — tue
hotel — hothal
mudguard — madgar
certificate — satikpitik
washer — asar
motor — matar
duty — dipti
conductor — contector
high court — hai kaut
safety pin — siptipin
burner — barnet
switch — such

It may be noted that 'tiffin carrier' becomes 'tifin kari' though, as has been mentioned above, 'carrier' becomes 'kariat'. Significantly, the motor-cycle is called 'bhatbhati' in Kurmali – the sound produced by the thing giving it the name. It should be pointed out here that names of certain things in Kurmali appear to be loan renditions from English bearing in mind the use of the things as known to the speakers. 'Loud-speaker' is 'kal gawna' *i.e.* the song machine. Apparently, the idea that loudspeakers could be used for other purposes also was not known to them, as can be guessed, when the name was given to it. 'Aeroplane' is likewise called 'ura jahaj' ('fly plane').

A close study of the proverbs and sayings used in Kurmali reveals that some of them have their origins in English — they appear to be more or less literal translations or loan renditions from English.

As is apparent from the above study, many things have been borrowed from English into Kurmali and, in fact, the impact is noticeable enough. It is true, however, that no easily perceptible pattern is to be seen. Evidently, Kurmali (as also other languages of the area) has had to admit new words descriptive of the new scene. Undoubtedly, these English words have entered Kurmali lexicon (and those of other tribal languages) through Hindi and many of them, as we have seen, have retained the forms in which they are used in Hindi. It is apparently a safe minimum to conclude that in all these languages the same tendencies have been generally at work as in Hindi.

REFERENCES

Abercrombie, D. 1967, *Elements of General Phonetics,* Edinburgh University Press.

Cohen, A. 1965, *The Phonemes of English,* The Hague, Martinus Nijhotf.

Mahato, K. 1982, *Kurmali Bhakhik Etihas Rup Chis*, Purulia, Savitri Press.

Prasad, B.N. and Shastri, Sudhakar Jha, 1958, Linguistic Survey of Southern Division of Manbhum and Dalbhum.

Sabzwari, S. 1975, *Urdu Lesaniyat,* Aligarh, Educational Book House.

Sethi, J. 1980, *Consonant Clusters in Educated Punjani-Speakers' English,* CIEFL Bulletin, Vol. 16, No. 1.

Singh, H.N., *Kurmali Boli Ke Muhavre aur Lokoktiyan,* Ranchi, Kurmali Bhasha Parishad.

Vidyarthi, V.S. 1967, *Kurmali Bhasha aur Sahitya, in Bhasha,* June 1967, Central Hindi Directorate, Ministry of Education, Government of India.